Flatmates and Bad Dates

HELEN BEAU *and* **LINDSAY BROM**

Copyright © Helen Beau and Lindsay Brom 2024

All rights reserved. No part of this publication may be reproduced, distributed, or transmitted in any form or by any means, including photocopying, recording, or other electronic or mechanical methods, without the prior written permission of the authors, except in the case of brief quotations embodied in critical reviews and certain other non-commercial uses permitted by copyright law. For permission requests, please contact the authors.'

Any resemblance to actual persons, living or dead, or actual events is purely coincidental. Names, characters, businesses, organizations, places, events, and incidents are either the product of the author's imagination or used fictitiously. Any resemblance to actual persons, living or dead, or actual events is entirely coincidental.

To all the women who've had to sit through countless crappy dates: We feel you. Embrace who you are and let each experience guide your growth. Try not to entertain Mr. Bare Minimum, Mr. Billy Big Balls, or Mr. I Don't Know What I Want —focus on finding Mr. Make It Happen, who you deserve.

In the meantime, enjoy dating for all the weird and wonderful stories it creates. These moments are part of your beautiful life story and can bring plenty of laughter to you and your friends along the way.

Helen and Lindsay xx

Contents

Chapter 1.   Lucy.....................................1
Chapter 2.   Layla....................................12
Chapter 3.   Scandal and London Dreams 18
Chapter 4.   The Rented Reality 21
Chapter 5.   From Colleagues to Housemates 24
Chapter 6.   Moving House on the Tube 34
Chapter 7.   The Mill Hill East Squatter 39
Chapter 8.   Ticket to Trouble: A Costly Shortcut...43
Chapter 9.   Teddy Ruxpin and Rubber Johnny 47
Chapter 10. Flat Hunting and Pub Brawls:
             Settling into Stoke Newington 64
Chapter 11. Blame It on the Cardigan.............78
Chapter 12. Gingerbread Man 90
Chapter 13. The Elephants Upstairs 102
Chapter 14. King-Ding-a-Long 115

Chapter 15.	Treading on Thin Ice 128
Chapter 16.	Shrek and Spok 147
Chapter 17.	The Big Election 159
Chapter 18.	Big Jacket 168
Chapter 19.	Fart Test and Food Poisoning 179
Chapter 20.	Dancing Queens 193
Chapter 21.	Fireman's Lift 202
Chapter 22.	Bring Your Own Bottle 216
Chapter 23.	South of the River 230
Chapter 24.	Crack the Whip 250
Chapter 25.	Studio Life 263
Chapter 26.	Kiss My Arse 273

Chapter One

Lucy

If my twenties had a soundtrack, it would have a mix of 'Blame It on the Alcohol' and 'I Will Survive'—with a special bonus track titled 'How Did I End Up in This Mess?'

But, before you are taken down memory lane, allow me to gracefully introduce myself. I am Lucy, a red wine enthusiast, with a fondness for blending half a teaspoon of coffee into my daily cups of tea—a concoction I affectionately call 'cof-tea.'

Once, in a moment of snack-time desperation, I slapped a slice of cheddar cheese on a Weetabix, and to my surprise, it wasn't half bad. You can thank me later.

This book, however, isn't about my odd eating habits; it's more of an example of how not to do things.

Let me start from the very beginning…

I had a lovely childhood in a small market town called Market Deeping, nestled just 8 miles from both Peterborough in Cambridgeshire and Stamford in Lincolnshire. Many people haven't heard of Market Deeping, so I often found myself explaining its location.

To simplify things, I sometimes explained that I lived in a small market town near Stamford, Stamford is known for being quite upmarket. Or I would say that I lived near Peterborough if I wanted a conversation starter about being close by to one of Britain's worst cities. A title it 'proudly' held three years in a row starting in 2018.

Originally born in Southampton and living in Lymington, we relocated to Market Deeping when I was a sweet and innocent six-year-old. My sister, just eighteen months older, was quite different from me in personality—like chalk and cheese—but we got along well.

Our parents, both teachers and wonderful individuals, supported every hobby my sister and I pursued. From twirling on ice to galloping on horses, tapping our way through dance classes, and creating symphonies on the piano, our childhood was full of varied interests.

We lived in a cul-de-sac, where my sister and I would play Kirby, Stuck in the Mud, Duck-Duck-Goose, and other traditional 1980s games with the neighbourhood children.

One of my best friends, Sally, lived across the road. We spent countless summer days playing in her garden sprinkler and pretending our bikes were horses, using sticks as whips for our imaginary horse-riding lessons. Childhood was very innocent.

But then, cue the teenage tornado when I was introduced to Mad-Dog 2020 and white lightning cider, which created sips of rebellion in the local park. Suddenly, a weekend spent horse-riding didn't seem so thrilling.

I plucked my eyebrows so thin you could hardly see them and started wearing make-up—heather shimmer lipstick, blue eyeshadow, and ghost-white foundation — I rolled my school skirt up so high to make a 'mini-skirt' that a teacher once told me (as I was being sent out of the classroom) to 'Get a new skirt; I can see your knickers.' I should have been embarrassed, but I wasn't at all. Quite proud of my make-shift new skirt, really.

My parents wouldn't buy me a short skirt (they wanted me to look classy), which I totally get now. But when we are teenagers, we never see things through our parents' eyes.

After finishing school, I was uncertain about my future; the only thing I knew for sure was that I wanted to leave. I had no clear sense of identity and was struggling to find my place in the world. In an attempt to reinvent myself, I dyed my naturally brunette hair to blonde, and I had it cut into a stylish slanted bob. I finally felt glamourous.

I took the summer off, and just before my 17th birthday in September, I landed a job at a call centre for an advertising company in Peterborough.

With an annual salary of £12,000, I felt like I was 'rolling-in-it.'

After purchasing a Mega Rider bus pass to commute into Peterborough Monday to Friday, I had nearly £900 a month to spend, and I couldn't believe it. At almost 17 years of age, I had never had so much money in my bank account before.

I would often treat friends to clothes from the Freemans catalogue cos I felt like I was rich and wanted to 'share the wealth.'

For a while I really enjoyed working at the advertising company because I met my friend Tara there.

At 22, she was five years older than me—petite, brunette, very pretty, and incredibly friendly and fun.

We hit it off immediately and became inseparable both at work and outside of it.

My first work event was at The Haycock in Stamford. Tara and I had pre-drinks at her house, and by the time we arrived at The Haycock by taxi, we were embarrassingly pissed.

We went straight to the stage above the dance floor to show off our dance moves. After a few dances, I stumbled, fell off the stage and lay flat on my face on the cold wooden floor.

Clearly, I didn't learn anything from being a drunken-mess at a work-do, because a few months later we had an awards event, at the posh Orton Hall Hotel in Peterborough and predictably, we got smashed again before we even arrived.

Tara wore a red dress that worked perfectly with her dark hair, while I had squeezed into a tight black satin number.

We both had trim figures, though I always had an extra-large behind—so much so, that at school one boy told me that I looked like a duck and proceeded to do impressions of me waddling along the corridor whilst sticking his bum out.

Tara and I, fully aware that we weren't in the running for any awards, decided to liven things up a bit.

While the speeches droned on and trophies were handed out, we snuck off from our tables to bounce and giggle-away on the bouncy castle in the background.

No one was impressed, but we were unaware and in our own drunken bubble. This was until one of the top managers stormed over and angrily ushered us off the bouncy castle, ordering us to return to our tables.

That wasn't enough mischief for one night. After our fun was taken away, we bided our time through the boring speeches by exchanging glances and mimicking exaggerated yawns to one another to keep ourselves entertained.

Once the DJ started playing music while everyone else was finishing their coffees, Tara and I decided to liven up the party.

Though there was no karaoke planned for the evening, we couldn't resist the urge to perform. So, we asked the DJ if we could borrow his microphone and requested 'Can't Fight the Moonlight' by LeAnn Rimes. The DJ obliged, and we took to the stage, dancing and singing for the entire advertising company, CEO and all. We truly put the fun into dysfunctional.

That fitted, satin dress that wasn't fit for someone with a larger behind eventually gave-up on me and after too much dancing - my dress split down the back from the middle all the way to the back of my knees, leaving my knickers on full display to the dance floor.

Not wanting to go home, I made my way to reception and the nice lady working there gave me some safety pins to pin it back together. I tried to make a replica of the 'Liz-Hurley' iconic Versace safety pin dress from the 1990's.

It wasn't impressive like hers, and you could still see my knickers.

After a year, I was bored of working in a call-centre and decided to enrol in a course at Peterborough College, where I delved into Journalism and Media Studies.

This chapter of my life was where I encountered my first serious boyfriend, we moved in together and I nestled into the city life of Peterborough.

As studies wrapped up (and so did that relationship), I found myself standing at the crossroads of uncertainty.

The gateway to the glamorous world of media beckoned, and what was my ticket in? A quirky TV shopping channel, with its headquarters conveniently planted in Peterborough that had a few spots open for 'Buying Assistants.'

It seemed like my golden ticket to bigger and better things – a chance to turn my love of purchasing into a real-life shopping spree of opportunities. Oh, the adventure that awaited!

When I got the job and started working there, reality hit harder than a failed online shopping spree when I realized that life at the TV Shopping Channel was far from the glamourous workplace I had envisioned.

Despite my blood, sweat, and occasional tears, my boss, Cassie who I nicknamed 'Cass-hole' (not to her face) had a peculiar obsession with my timekeeping.

One minute late? Cue the monthly HR parade. On time? Into a room I'd go, receiving a disdainful look for daring to arrive precisely at 9 am. Never mind the fact that I'd stay an extra hour after my shift, or skip lunch when work became chaotic.

Cass-hole, the ultimate jobs worth, had me henpecked and I was loathing every minute of it.

And then, there was the infamous 'Chile' incident. In all innocence, I asked Cass-hole where 'Chile' was, confidently pronouncing it just as it looks — rhyming with 'smile.' I was immediately met with a disgusted glare. Little did I know, in South America, it's pronounced 'chee-lay.'

Who knew? Certainly not me. Geography wasn't exactly my favourite subject at school. Cass-hole's sour-faced reaction was absurd, she was such a miserable cow. If I were in her shoes, I'd have found it downright hilarious. But alas, laughter was non-existent in the kingdom of my disgruntled boss.

The job, in all its degrading glory then reached new heights of absurdity.

Cass-hole took pleasure in showcasing my awkwardness, selecting me (and only me) to interrupt crucial meetings with ongoing presentations to enquire if the 'important' folks desired a coffee.

It pissed me off, I wasn't hired to be a waitress and no-one else in our department was ever asked to do this!

The request was never enthusiastically received. Cass-hole's power trip was evident to all, and even the coffee-seeking managers couldn't mask it; thankfully they all said that they didn't require a coffee, much to Cass-hole's disappointment.

I did once take Cass-hole to HR over her 'nit-picking' behaviour, but nothing got done and it only made the strain between her and I worse. It even gave her another opportunity to discuss with HR how I never arrive at my desk at least 5 minutes before my shift starts. In my defence, that wasn't a requirement in my contract.

The company was not bad, the job was not bad; it was my boss who made the place seem unbearable. But as miserable as this was, I would not change it for only one reason. This is how I became friends with Layla.

Layla – a lively character straight out of our shared hometown of Market Deeping. We both hailed from the same turf, breathing in the local air of small-town familiarity.

Layla, a few years ahead of me in school, had already secured her status as one of the 'cool' girls in her batch.

And after my school years had wrapped up, our paths occasionally crossed at the Coach House and The Stage, the go-to pubs for us 'Deepingers.'

I knew Layla by sight, a familiar face in the crowd, but our interactions were just a nod, a smile, and the unspoken acknowledgment that we shared a slice of this humble hometown pie.

Until we worked together at the TV Shopping Channel. Layla worked there as a Merchandising Assistant. We recognised one another from Market Deeping and would say hello. But then it turned into daily emails to meet one another at the photocopier, and photocopy blank pieces of paper to pretend we were working so we could gossip about life in Deeping, men and how we both had a desire to move to London.

I often spent my time dreaming of moving to London, but unsure whether it would ever come to fruition, I bought my first house in Peterborough at the age of 22.

Putting my dreams on hold I spent some weekends taking the train and exploring the London nightlife. After years of partying in Peterborough, this new experience was a very welcome change.

In Peterborough, I had a side-gig as a columnist for a local magazine, dishing out pearls of wisdom on health and beauty.

It was one of the highlights of the time I spent in the City of Peterborough because I had a trusty little press pass, and I could breeze into the VIP sections of nightclubs like a wizard opening secret doors.

And let's face it, who doesn't love a VIP pass to every nightclub in town? I loved every minute of it. Apart from the time someone recognised me from my column and called me a 'dick.'

The nightlife in Peterborough had loads of great bars and clubs back in its glory days. But still, I was yearning for a breath of fresh air for my social and work life, in a place called London.

Chapter Two

Layla

I'm Layla, and I have a love for rosé wine, aloe vera, and showing off my party trick of standing on my head—especially when I'm pissed. Because who doesn't want to see a tipsy woman attempt amateur acrobatics?

I don't have a middle-name, unlike all of my friends that seemed to have one. So, I used to tell people that my middle name was Jane.

My childhood was a happy one. I grew up in Market Deeping, the only place I had ever known as home. My parents hailed from Nottingham, and although they never envisioned life in a quiet market town, a bank promotion prompted their move, nudging them away from the city they cherished.

Embracing small-town life and having high aspirations for me, they urged me to focus, to excel in school, and they spoke about their dreams for me to go to university.

Unfortunately for them that was not to be the case. School was more of a social setting for me, I barely did any work and spent most of my time hanging around the back of the school underneath the leisure centre steps and smoking cigarettes. Detention was a regular thing, and parents evening usually carried the theme of 'she has such great potential, if only she would use it.'

Much like Lucy, most of my weekends as a teenager consisted of drinking underage in various locations—fields, parks, friends' houses, and the local leisure centre. My friendship circle was a group of girls who were well-known around the school for all the wrong reasons.

While their reputation had a cool status, and even though I hung around with them, I was the least cool of the group. But back in those days, you were simply happy to be accepted in a popular group.

My sister's then-boyfriend, a character teetering on the edge of shadiness, once played the role of our spirits supplier. At the tender age of thirteen, my friends and I eagerly embarked on an adventure with a bottle of Thunderbird, with fumes reminiscent of petrol.

Surprisingly, I, the un-cool kid wary of overindulgence, tried to keep my composure. However,

I ended up eventually guzzling down the bottle and succumbed to a drunken state. Although one of my friends, was much worse than me.

As my very drunk friend wobbled around the streets, she became prime prey for undercover police on the prowl looking for underage drinkers; the Leisure Centre in Market Deeping was notorious for us all getting off-our-heads around there.

My friend was ushered away in a police car, leaving me and our other friend hiding in a local field and concocting wild scenarios about her police encounter.

The following day, believing I had dodged the bullet, the police came knocking at my parents' door. Sworn to secrecy not to reveal the source of our alcohol supplier, I stumbled through a half-hearted tale of an unknown teenager buying the forbidden juice for us.

Ironically, my friend had lenient parents, and she emerged unscathed, allowing her back out again the following week. In contrast, I faced the measures of grounding, coupled with a stern chat to avoid the Leisure Centre on Friday nights.

By the time I hit sixteen, the fear of my parents' disapproval vanished, and I openly embraced a regular routine of drinking around the neighbourhood, casting aside any lingering dreams of academic success for a life of booze and boys. Life, it seemed, had become one grand, rebellious party, and giving my middle finger to anything beyond my social life.

My departure from school was marked by a pitiful three GCSEs, and I headed off to college to do what I later found out was referred to as 'the dropouts' course, 'Leisure and Tourism.' In my defence, my choice stemmed from dreams of an adventurous career abroad.

However, fate had other plans when I encountered my first boyfriend. He was a typical 'bad-boy,' and like most things in my life, any distraction to take me away from being on a well-trodden path was always welcomed with open arms.

The distraction saw me barely scraping through college, and at one point I got kicked off the course and had to go back into college over the summer to finish it.

The tale of my turbulent love life continued well into my early twenties, living with my 'bad-boy' boyfriend and the addition of a Jack Russell named Charlie. Only for it all to come to an ugly end, but thankfully I had come to my senses and knew it was for the best.

Ironically, the very 'dropouts' course that contributed to my academic detour eventually played a pivotal role in fulfilling my dream of working abroad. Accepted as a Thompson representative, I embarked on a season in Majorca, although the enthusiasm of overseas work faded quickly, revealing a reality less glamorous than the fun life I had imagined.

With a ticket in hand, I made my way back to the familiar surroundings of my parents' home, finding myself once again in the comfort of my old bedroom.

The next three years were spent in and out of various shitty admin jobs around the local area, and then I ended up at the TV Shopping Channel where I met Lucy.

Following a stint of cohabiting with a boyfriend at this point – an experience best left unexplored, as it abruptly ended after I came home one night from Central Nightclub in Stamford to find my clothes being thrown out of our bedroom window and onto the front lawn for all the neighbours to see.

I found myself once again living back with my parents.

LUCY

They caution about the company we as individuals keep, urging us to select friends who complement our flaws.

Perhaps there was a slight hiccup going on in the universe on the day Layla and I forged our friendship connection.

It's like one fuck up leading the other fuck up.

What could possibly go wrong?

To find out, let's time travel to 2008.

Chapter Three

Scandal and London Dreams

January 2008

LUCY

The daily grind in the offices at The TV Shopping Channel turned into a crime thriller when I realized Layla had mysteriously disappeared from the workplace scene. Naturally, my curiosity got the best of me, and I embarked on a mission to uncover the scandalous truth.

After some 'expert-level detective work (aka casually asking someone in her department), I learned that Layla got the boot. The reason? Layla, the mastermind, sent some emails featuring less-than-flattering images of Barry from Eastenders to a colleague, suggesting that he looked like their boss. I couldn't help but laugh; this would be a classic Layla move in her ever-dramatic life.

Her boss, apparently moonlighting as Sherlock Holmes, had their emails snooped on by the IT squad. Shockingly, they weren't thrilled to find themselves in the midst of Layla's mischief and the boss swiftly lodged a complaint with HR.

Layla, not one to go down without a fight, countered the allegations and told HR all about the bald boss and his unsolicited advances during a work trip. In the end, both Layla and the boss got the axe.

And just like that, the daily gossip sessions with Layla came to a screeching halt... or so I believed.

Layla, a go-with-the-flow kind of girl, laid-back and without set plans, following life wherever it takes her. The kind of person who turns life's little disasters into spontaneous adventures. With her dark-brown bob haircut and air of mystery, she was always ready to embrace whatever came her way. So, I couldn't predict what her new plans would be.

However, a moon or two later, word 'on the street' (Layla's ex colleague) was that Layla pulled off a London calling of her own and snagged a plum position with a fancy-schmancy fashion brand. My initial reaction? Pure happiness for her! Yet, my excitement was met with a cold shoulder in the form of unanswered texts.

I figured she was knee-deep in the fabulous chaos of London living, the glamorous London life we used to dream about by the photocopier. As her absence lingered, the office lost a dash of fun. No more infectious giggles, no more tales of Layla's weekend dramas – it was like a silent vacuum in our once fast-paced, lively workplace. The TV Shopping Channel felt a bit lacklustre without Layla's spark.

But hey, credit where it's due, she did exactly what she vowed to do: a London move, and I was so proud of her. As I admired her gutsy leap, I couldn't help but catch a whiff of inspiration.

Perhaps, just perhaps, a London adventure was on my horizon too. One day, I thought, as I daydreamed of my own chapter in the big city of London.

Chapter Four

The Rented Reality

LAYLA

Before I'd been sacked from the TV Shopping Channel, I had already secured a job in London. With my relationship ending, I wasted no time in looking to move to London.

Searching Gumtree, the only piece of the puzzle left was to find a decent place to live. A male friend suggested looking at a place in the London Borough of Hackney called Stoke Newington. With no preconceptions, I gladly accepted that this would be a suitable place to live.

With a busy high street boasting chic cafes, a quirky strip of bars, indie shops, and restaurants, I knew this place would suit me and give me the experience of settling into London Life.

After hours of scouring Gumtree for housing options, I stumbled upon a room in a flat in this area, a perfect arrangement at £450 a month, bills included. The male and female already living there were sub-letting to me, which I was not aware of at the time.

It was only after I moved in that I realized why the room was so cheap. It seemed very professional at first, signed a contract and all. Yet, the room had a pungent smell of dampness, a broken window above my bed that refused closure, and it backed onto a dark, eerie alleyway.

Yet, in keeping with the recurring theme of my life so far, I gritted my teeth and embraced the situation.

A few days after I moved in, I started my new job. The job, in contrast, was a world away from my mouldy flat that I was stepping out of the door from every morning. I was working for a luxury fashion brand in Soho, Central London, with most of my colleagues living a more affluent lifestyle.

While my role was not in design but on the technical side, conducting audits on the company's production sites, a stroke of luck had me stationed on their design floor. This provided me with a front-row seat to the creative heartbeat of the brand.

Initially overwhelmed and painfully shy, I kept my head low, feeling like a fish out of water. However, as time unfolded, I began forging connections, making friends, and throwing myself into the London culture.

The post-work scenes in and around Soho, with numerous drinks, rendered me a bona fide Londoner. One particular friend, also single, became my sidekick, and we had many nights of getting hammered, which I was happy to do, not wanting to go back to the depressing flat I was currently living in.

On the occasions when I had to head straight home from work, I would make a pit stop at the local off-licence, grab a few beers, and perch myself in Clissold Park, biding my time until my weed-smoking, cliquey flatmates had retired for the night. This was the downside of living in London that I hadn't imagined. Hoping that I would have moved into a place where I could become friends with my flatmates. But this was not my reality.

Amidst my drunken adventures in London, I found myself phoneless after a wild night out. After about a week or so, and armed with a new mobile phone and number, I made my way to an internet café to log into my personal emails. It was time to update everyone with my new digits and reply to the concerned emails, reassuring them that, yes, I was still alive.

Chapter Five

From Colleagues to Housemates

LUCY

After feeling inspired by Layla's move to London. I spent a few evenings tossing my CV into the abyss of London job applications, a glimmer of hope emerged when I snagged an interview for the position of assistant buyer at the head office of a high street retail giant nestled just off the bustling lanes of Oxford Street.

This was the kind of job that could easily be the dream of at least fifty other ambitious people across the country – perhaps ones armed with fashion degrees and a quirky fashion-sense.

The interview process demanded more than just a well-pressed suit; I had to showcase fashion awareness by crafting a trend board predicting the upcoming styles for autumn 2008. Now, being the procrastinator that I am, preparation was never my forte.

In the eleventh hour, I scrambled together clippings from glossy magazines, creating a trend board that, let's be honest, was a tad shit. But with my less-than-perfect creation tucked under my arm, I tried to imagine that I would be carrying this 'Trend Board' like a ticket to a world of professionalism, and I couldn't shake the sensation of hoping and praying that I was on the verge of something big.

Suddenly I couldn't unsee, that soon this girl from a small market town could be transformed into an actual London professional. I pictured myself armed with a takeaway coffee and striding confidently through the bustling streets of London. The prospect of the big city as my playground, the promise of exciting opportunities – I was nervous with anticipation.

So, there I was, on the day of my crucial interview, caught in the chaos of London's rush hour. I had to get from Peterborough's train station to King's Cross station, then onto the underground and onto the Victoria line to get to Oxford Circus– the place for my professional dreams.

It was 7.30 am, and the tube was crammed with bodies, an intimate encounter with humanity as we were squeezed together like sardines. I'm squished in, face nestled into a stranger's armpit (luckily it was a nice smelling armpit) and clinging to the pole for dear life because there's not a seat in sight. This wasn't the glamorous tube journey in rush hour I had dreamed of.

So, there I was on the tube, minding my own business, squished to the left of me was this absolute vision of professionalism. You know the type: pixie haircut, sleek thin-framed glasses, the works. She looked like she was on her way to negotiate world peace or at least run a very important PowerPoint presentation.

Anyway, as the tube screeched to a halt at Oxford Circus and the doors slid open, people started to disembark, including Miss Professional. But just as I was about to step out, she steps on the edge of my right shoe, I stumbled out of the tube doors and my shoe went flying back off my foot like a missile through the crowded tube. It all happened so fast, that I didn't fully grasp what had happened until I was stood on the platform and missing a shoe.

When I did fully realize that I needed to spring into action, the crowds of people then spilling into the tube and kicking my shoe further down the tube made it impossible for me to dart back on and reclaim it before the tube doors slammed shut again. The tube departed, leaving my shoe on its own little adventure to who-knows-where.

I hobbled off down the platform to exit the station with a tint blushing my face. I wasn't sure whether to laugh about the awful situation or cry. How was I going to turn up to an interview with only one shoe and my chipped nail polish on display?

No shops were opening until 9 a.m., and my interview was at 8:15 a.m. I was in full-on panic mode, standing outside the station with one lonely shoe and no clue what to do.

In a moment of sheer desperation, I spotted a homeless man outside the tube station and contemplated asking him if I could borrow his holey, worn-out boots. They appeared to be about five sizes too big for me and they looked like they'd been through a few World Wars, but at least I'd have a pair if he would let me!

The idea of clomping into the interview like a toddler in their dad's shoes seemed marginally less humiliating than showing up with just one shoe on. But then I chickened out, too embarrassed to even ask.

So instead, I hobbled off in search of Scrabble Street where the office of my dreams was located. It was a street around the corner from Wimpole Street, a ten-minute walk from Oxford Circus station.

And as I stepped into the office that I was being interviewed in I felt a wave of disappointment. This place was nothing like the sleek, glamorous interior I had imagined—no resemblance to the chic, polished offices from *The Devil Wears Prada*.

Instead, I found myself in a dingy, colourless, and worn-out building that barely hinted at the vibrant world of fashion. It wasn't the fashion house of my dreams, but then again, we all have to start somewhere, right? And who was I to be judgemental when I was turning up to an interview with the loss of one shoe, a dirty right foot and 20% of my dignity?

The Head of Buying greeted me, and we both burst out laughing about my one-shoe wonder act. She admitted that this was hands down the funniest start to an interview she'd ever had. I joked that I was happy to be of comedy service and hoped that this would make a memorable impression, figuring this might work in my favour—no chance of her forgetting me now, right?

She told me that she would dig out some size 4s from the fashion samples for me to keep after my interview. She was lovely, and my knight in shining stilettos in that moment.

She led me to her tiny office, tucked away at the back of the main buying area. As we walked through, I had to pass by rows of people at their desks, all of them pausing mid-email to look up and stare at the spectacle that was me—one shoe on and doing a great impression of a wonky donkey. I kept my head down, praying that my cheeks weren't as red as they felt. My barefoot made a sad little shuffle sound with every step, almost like it knew how ridiculous I looked.

The Head of Buying was probably in her late forties, tall, with shoulder-length blonde hair. Dressed in jeans and a crisp white blouse, she had a classic yet trendy look. She looked very well put together, a complete contrast from my look of a plain black pencil dress and one shoe—hardly the sort of outfit that screamed 'hire me now.' I hoped that my trend board would do the talking, proving that I had a keen eye for style, even if my outfit didn't reflect it that day.

The interview turned out to be easier than I expected, more of a friendly chat than a grilling. It seemed to go well, and she appeared impressed with my hastily 'put together' trend board creation. However, she was so lovely that it was hard to gauge whether I had truly made a good impression.

After my interview I left with my new shoes on my feet as promised, and whilst making my way back to Peterborough, I got a phone call from an unknown number. I snagged the job! My giddy excitement could only be rivalled by the thought of sharing the news with Layla.

But alas, technological barriers thwarted my attempts; texts went unanswered, and I was not on any form of social media at this point, so I had no way of reaching out. Layla proved elusive, and I had no other way of getting in touch with her.

I had a 4-week notice period at the TV Shopping Channel, and it was brilliant to see Cass-hole's surprised face as I handed in my letter of resignation. Although she looked relieved that I was leaving. I wasn't offended cos the feeling was mutual - we both knew that this hell of working together was finally over. The things I would have loved to have written in that letter, but I remained professional, and besides I needed a good reference.

I was still gutted that I couldn't reach Layla. But one morning in the office, there was an unexpected hero in the form of a breathless ex-colleague of Layla's, frantically waving a paper like a triumphant messenger pigeon.

Emma, who had worked on the same team as Layla, had reached out to her via email, learning of my London-bound adventure during my notice at the TV Shopping Channel. She passed her digits to Emma, who, in turn, raced to me with Layla's new contact details.

Happiness washed over me; I now had a London girlie friend before even stepping foot in the city.

That evening after work, as soon as the sanctuary of home embraced me, I dialled Layla's number. Plans were swiftly made to meet up. We agreed to meet up after my first day in my new job. By now I had a week left at the shopping channel and a farewell work party at Edwards Bar in Peterborough.

As the week wrapped up and the weekend arrived, my leaving party commenced. Around twenty people showed up, and for some reason, a red carpet had been laid out in front of the bar that evening (not for me).

My friend Rick, whom I had previously met from the TV Shopping Channel, was ecstatic about this. He was obsessed with becoming a celebrity and walking the red carpet—even if it was just outside a bar in Peterborough where no one knew who he was.

Once, someone had told Rick that he looked like Declan Donnelly, so he changed his Facebook profile picture to Declan. I'm not sure why—maybe he hoped that others would also see the resemblance and it would make him feel like a celebrity, even if he was just an imposter.

Anyway, Rick insisted on having pictures taken of us walking arm-in-arm on the red carpet. My friend Kerrie stood at the side, pretending to be paparazzi, and snapped lots of pictures. I, of course, obliged, finding the whole situation very entertaining. Who was I to kill Rick's one moment on the red carpet?

Rick was always great fun to be around, he had an infectious humour, flamboyant and he was a brilliant friend. I had pegged him as gay, but his love for finding a nice woman hinted otherwise. Regardless, Rick was my perfect but not-perfect, gay-but-not-gay best friend.

On the Monday after a weekend recovering from my work leaving do, I was straight into commuting to London for my new job. My first day went really well, but I couldn't wait for the day to be over so I could go and meet Layla. Layla greeted me outside the hallowed grounds of the old Topshop on Oxford Street. Dressed in a red chequered shirt and skinny black jeans she looked slimmer than ever. London living looked good on her.

Little did I know, in the midst of our catching up, Layla dropped a bombshell – a bizarre living situation that she had got herself into. She proposed the idea of us becoming housemates.

Layla, discontent with her current living arrangements, yearned for an escape. I spilled the beans by text to Rick, who was currently commuting to London from Cambridge and now working for a production company. Rick and I had already agreed to find a place together as he was sick of the commute, and he was on board with the plan for Layla to join us in a house-share too.

So, there it was, a pact sealed amidst the bustling streets of Oxford Street – the three musketeers, or in our case, the three-bedroom housemates, ready to embark on the next chapter of our lives in the heart of London.

With the unwavering support of my parents, they helped me to rent out my Peterborough house and assist Layla, Rick, and me with our house-hunting in London. They stumbled upon the perfect haven in Mill Hill East – a charming 4-bedroom detached house that surpassed my expectations, especially given our limited funds.

As the ink dried on the deposit check, we took to Gumtree, casting a net for the ideal housemate to fill our extra room that we hadn't anticipated.

Enter Sam, a chap working in the heart of Central London, who answered our advert. A meet-and-greet sealed the deal, and in no time, we found ourselves embarking on this cohabitation adventure: Me, Layla, Rick, and Sam.

The last leg of my commuting ordeal, shuttling between Peterborough and London was exhausting. Weight loss became an unexpected side effect of the relentless walking and hurrying. Rising at 4 am and retiring at 9 pm every night, the glamour of London life for me wasn't this and I couldn't wait to move down there permanently especially since we had secured a place.

Chapter Six

Moving House on the Tube

LAYLA

Five months of living in the city of London had been a rollercoaster with my peculiar Gumtree-sourced flatmates, and I was more than ready to trade weird for familiarity and move in with Lucy.

I decided to pull a disappearing act on my flatmates because, let us face it, breaking up is hard to do, especially when it comes to shared tenancy agreements. I had this irrational fear that if I uttered the words 'I'm outta here,' some magical contract fairy would appear, waving a wand,

and boom! I would be legally bound to stay with my quirky flatmates forever.

So, in true ninja fashion, I sneaked around the apartment while they were earning their daily bread, strategically stuffing my belongings into bags. I tiptoed my way to the tube station with my vintage 1980's style TV in-hand, hoping to make a grand escape before anyone noticed.

Not the most conventional way to move through a bustling London underground with my worldly belongings; most people hire a van, get a taxi, or at least get a lift from a friend. But in typical Layla style and feeling like a DIY guru of the relocation world, I wade, carrying my entire existence and, a bulky vintage TV.

I hopped off at Euston, feeling like I had cracked the code to the London Underground treasure map. Next stop, Mill Hill East. As I transitioned from the underground to the overground and arrived at Mill Hill East, a profound question hit me: 'Where in this universe do I live now?'

But the adventure was not over. Oh no, the house, my new sanctuary, was a good 20-minute walk from the station, it might as well have been on another planet. When viewing the place, it didn't seem too far, but as I dragged my belongings, TV in tow, down the hill, the strain started setting in.

In a moment of contemplation, I pondered leaving the TV on the curb, hoping someone with a time machine to the '80s might appreciate the gesture. But, just then, like a Fiesta-shaped fairy godmother, two guys pulled up, offering me a lift. I accepted.

Now, if normal folks were handed a red flag at the idea of hitching a ride with strangers, they would turn tail and run. But me? I am on a first-name basis with never doing anything quite the 'norm.' At this stage, my journey was already slightly odd anyway and the fear of extended walking had overtaken any rational concerns about jumping into a car with the Ford Fiesta dudes.

Luckily for me, my new chauffeurs were not mad rapists or serial killers, just your run-of-the-mill, surprisingly normal guys. They dumped me right at my doorstep, and as I stepped out of their car with all my possessions, a massive sigh of relief escaped me. Voilà! I had arrived, but I could not be bothered with unpacking. I had a night out planned.

Plans were in place for a night out with my friend Carl at the legendary Fabric nightclub in Farringdon, and nothing was going to rain on my parade.

I dumped my stuff in my new bedroom, unpacking only what I needed to quickly get ready, and I set foot out of the door to the tube station yet again, but this time feeling a lot lighter. Amidst the bustling chaos of Kings Cross Station, I encountered Carl, marking the start of an unforgettable night.

We navigated the tube to Farringdon, where our evening embarked with innocent intentions of only having a couple of drinks in a nearby cocktail bar to get us into the party mood. A couple turned into many, and we both ended up pretty hammered by the time we left the cocktail bar before heading to the club.

The queue at the club seemed eternal, but excitement energised our spirits. Inside, Carl's friends were there, with one of his mates catching my eye, leading to me following him around throughout the club in my intoxicated state, with grand delusions of something happening.

Once inside, a renowned DJ set the club ablaze (I cannot remember who now). I felt tired after an eventful day and following Carl's friend around the club, so I took myself away from Carl and collapsed onto one of Fabric's double beds, blissfully unaware of my surroundings and dribbling into the pillow.

I am not sure how long I was out for, but Carl jolted me into consciousness as he announced our shift to an after-party at the residence of my newfound crush. It all went a bit hazy from there, but I remember the party being wild with illegal substances passed around.

As dawn painted the sky and the party came to a halt, Carl and I head off and decided to get the bus back to my new pad in Mill Hill East. As we were over the river, the journey back seemed endless and when we finally made it back home, we both crashed out.

The next morning, I awaken to find Carl still asleep. I was hungry and dehydrated, so I ventured off in search of the local shop, hoping to get there and back before Lucy arrived to move in.

Chapter Seven

The Mill Hill East Squatter

August 2008

LUCY

The four weeks of daily train marathons eventually gave way to the eagerly anticipated moving day. My best mate Kerrie and her friend Paul offered to drive my belongings and me down to the big smoke. Packed snugly into Paul's van, we embarked on the journey to my new home.

Sausage rolls fuelled our journey, and the radio became our karaoke stage. Amidst the excitement, my lifelong best friend Kerrie wept, as she couldn't believe

I wouldn't be living up the road from her anymore. Our bond, forged since the tender age of six, faced the strain of separation. I was also going to miss her so much and I couldn't believe I would now be hours away from her, but my focus was still unwavering – London beckoned, promising a fresh chapter in my life, and nothing would divert my gaze from that horizon.

The charm of Mill Hill East greeted us as we rolled up to Cherry Tree Road, our new place of residence, filled with both excitement and unfamiliarity. At the end of the long street stretched the promise of a pub. Get in. The scene was set for a perfect beginning.

A mere 20-minute stroll away stood an overground tube stop, a convenient link to the heartbeat of the city.

Armed with a key from the estate agents, picked up the day before after work, I stood ready to unlock the door to our dreams.

Layla, already living in London, had moved in the day prior, while I patiently bided my time until the grand moving day on Saturday.

As the door creaked open, releasing a flood of aspirations, I decided to offer Kerrie and Paul the grand tour before the chaos of moving commenced. 'Hello!' I announced into the stillness of the hallway, met with an unexpected silence. Assuming Layla must be out somewhere.

The tour kicked off downstairs, and the approving glances from Kerrie and Paul spurred me on. Ascending to the first floor, I showcased Rick's room – a lovely double room with a bed provided. Rick was set to move in the day after me.

Next in line was Layla's spacious room. But then, an odd noise of movement and breathing was heard coming from the side of Layla's bed by the window. Was Layla playing hide and seek with us? The situation felt weird.

I turned to Kerrie and Paul 'Did you hear that?'

Before they could answer, a sudden eruption shattered the mystery as a towering 6ft 4 man shot up from the side of the bed.

I was so shocked – 'Who the hell are you?' I stammered out, only for the giant to reassure us, 'Hi, my name is Carl. It's okay, don't panic. I'm Layla's friend. She's just at the shops.'

My initial reaction slipped out with a muttered, 'I thought you were a squatter,' and I burst out laughing while Carl looked embarrassed.

However, as fate would have it, Paul and Carl were acquainted. They exchanged handshakes as if it were the most natural thing in the world – not a meeting with someone playing hide and seek down the side of a bed with Layla's new housemate.

Little did I know, this unexpected encounter marked the inception of not just a new life in London, but an adventure filled with unpredictable moments.

I realized at this moment I didn't quite 'know' Layla as well as I thought, but I was excited about what being housemates had in store. Especially if there were going to be more comedy moments like that.

Chapter Eight

Ticket to Trouble: A Costly Shortcut

LAYLA

It was very different moving from Stoke Newington in Zone 2 to Mill Hill East in Zone 4—a practical countryside to inner-city dwellers who rarely ventured beyond Zone 2! But there we were, in a spacious and delightful house, despite the lengthy commute. However, the journey to work turned out to be more costly. I'd not always been great with budgeting, and I frequently found myself without the fare for the Tube.

I thought I'd found a clever workaround. I'd tailgate Lucy through the ticket barrier, using her oyster card. Lucy, ever laid-back, didn't mind. After all, if we got caught, I'd be the one paying the penalty. The only snag was navigating through one of the busiest Tube stations in the West End—Oxford Circus—teeming with security staff. It was only a matter of time before someone caught on.

And, sure enough, a few weeks into our scheme, it happened. On a hectic Monday morning, as I squished in behind Lucy going through the barriers after she tapped her oyster card, three security guards appeared from nowhere and caught me in the act. My heart pounded like a drum. It was game over.

'Come with us, young lady,' one of the guards commanded. Lucy, bless her, was torn. She had to get to work but didn't want to leave me panic-stricken. I told her to go; it was my stupid idea after all.

I was escorted to a small, dingy station room, filled with surveillance monitors showing the bustling commuters. I felt like a fool for ever thinking this plan would work.

I tried to talk my way out of it, babbling some nonsense about losing my oyster card enroute. But I've never been good at lying on the spot. It made me feel like a prized twat that I honestly thought this was a good idea in the first place. The guards saw right through me. I received a stern lecture, a £50 on-the-spot fine, and I was late for work. It was a major pity party for one for the rest of the day.

The same week, on the Thursday evening I went for drinks with my work colleagues at a pub in Soho. It became a regular occurrence to head straight to a bar with a group from the office to blow off some steam if we'd had a stressful day.

This particular Thursday evening, I was reasonably intoxicated, left the pub alone, and wobbled off to the tube station to catch the Northern Line back to Mill Hill. As I've mentioned, it's a bit of a journey, and although I took this route daily, I wasn't exactly in the soundest frame of mind. The late-night tube was mostly empty, so I settled into a seat and got comfortable for the trip home. Somewhere along the way, I fell fast asleep.

I woke up at the end of the line, Totteridge and Whetstone. I had missed my stop at Finchley Central, where I was supposed to switch to a direct tube to Mill Hill East or catch a bus. Now, stranded and quite drunk in the early hours of the morning, I realized my options were limited.

A handsome random traveller informed me that only buses were running at this hour, and they weren't frequent. We had a bit of a flirt, and a laugh at my expense and swopped numbers before he went on his way. 'At least something exciting has come out of this journey,' I thought.

I found a nearby bus stop and hoped for the best. After waiting for about twenty minutes, a bus arrived. I got on, unsure if it would take me towards Mill Hill. The driver informed me, whilst on the trip that it did not. Feeling hopeless, I got off, knowing it would be daylight before I made it home, and I had work in the morning. I hopped on and off another bus, feeling increasingly useless. Eventually, a sympathetic driver asked, 'You okay, love? Where are you trying to get to?'

'Mill Hill,' I told him, hoping for some good news.

'Well, I'm going to Finchley Central, love,' he replied. Finally, I was getting closer to home. At Finchley Central, I either had to catch another bus or face a long walk. Lucky for me, a bus to Mill Hill was waiting. Tired, weary, and a little traumatized, I finally strolled through the door at 3 a.m.

The next morning, I woke up, and had a text message from the random traveller asking if I would like to meet for a drink after work. We agreed to meet at my local pub, at least this way I wouldn't encounter another nightmare journey home if the date went well.

The date didn't go well. The date was cut-short, after the random traveller asked if I wanted to see his Prince Albert under the table.

Chapter Nine

Teddy Ruxpin and Rubber Johnny

August 2008 – June 2009

LUCY

Layla and I wasted no time immersing ourselves in the local scene of Mill Hill East. One of our early encounters involved meeting two interesting characters, Rubber Johnny and Teddy Ruxpin. Rubber Johnny, a tall, blonde, and skinny guy, took a liking to me, but my feelings weren't reciprocated. We affectionately named him Rubber Johnny simply because his name was Johnny, with no other reason behind it. For the record, he didn't look like a condom. I mean, if he did, he would have been made for the world's largest ding-dong as Rubber Johnny was 6ft 2.

Teddy Ruxpin, on the other hand, was Rubber Johnny's friend who frequented the local pubs and took a liking to Layla. He was short, chubby, and had deep brown eyes that were almost circular – resembling a teddy bear from the Bear Factory. Layla's feelings weren't reciprocated either. Despite the absence of romantic sparks, we entertained the duo, seeing them as potential friends in the area.

One Friday evening, Layla and I orchestrated a get-together with Rubber Johnny and Teddy Ruxpin at the quaint local pub. While Rubber Johnny dutifully attended to his work behind the bar, Teddy Ruxpin was on the other side of the bar at a table with a group of rowdy lads. We joined the lively gathering at their table; drinks flowed into the evening, jokes cracked, and laughter filled the air.

Later on, all the lads (apart from Rubber Johnny) decided to go outside to smoke some weed, and Layla, being partial to a well-rolled spliff, decided to partake. Already under the influence of alcohol, the weed propelled her into a disoriented state, transforming her demeanour as she swayed from left to right, eventually reappearing inside the pub.

As closing time approached, Layla ventured upstairs to the pub toilet. As I snapped out of my drunken, wine-fuelled state, a lingering concern prompted me to embark on a search for her, sensing that she had been absent for an unusually long time.

As I cautiously stepped into the sanctuary of the ladies' toilets, my eyes widened at the sight of Layla's legs protruding from beneath a toilet cubicle. Panic surged through me, and I frantically called out to her, asking about her well-being. Silence followed. The door was locked, and I didn't know what to do.

Racing downstairs, I urgently summoned Rubber Johnny from behind the bar for assistance, envisioning catastrophic scenarios playing out in my mind—headline news, parental distress, the whole melodramatic spectacle.

Layla was 27 and despite being younger than her at 24, I felt a great sense of responsibility for her, and at this point I had realised that Layla was a bit of a liability at times.

Rubber Johnny rushed back upstairs with me, and together we pried open the cubicle to reveal a semi-conscious Layla having a nap on the floor. I woke her up, but she wasn't able to walk unaided. Rubber Johnny took on the role of hero, hoisting her over his shoulder and carrying her down the stairs. His heroic stint, however, was cut short as pub-closing duties beckoned, and he had to stay behind to clean and lock up.

Teddy Ruxpin's friend, the designated driver, whisked everyone else away in his car, leaving me outside the pub alone with Layla. She wasn't in a fit state to stand properly, swaying from side to side.

Attempts to flag down a taxi weren't happening; the drivers being wary of Layla's potential projectile vomit after looking at the state of her.

Left with no alternative, I embarked on the long, dreary trek down the road with Layla in tow supporting her dead weight and trying to get her to put one foot in front of the other.

She was reluctant to help me to help her, and in an attempt to lift her spirits for her to pick up her snail-pace, I unleashed a questionable rendition of Shania Twain's 'Man! I Feel Like a Woman.'

Regrettably, Layla, gaining an unexpected burst of energy, incorporates a kick of the leg dance move so high that led to her falling backwards on the pavement. She bursts into uncontrollable laughter assuring me she was ok.

After what felt like an eternity we were safely home, she fell asleep by the front door, while I, weary and exasperated left her curled up in a ball so that I could go and put on my pyjamas.

After putting on my pyjamas I wanted to go to bed, but guilt set in for leaving her by the front door. Especially as Sam wasn't home and the thought of him having to step over her late at night wouldn't have been nice for either of them.

So, I went to check on her whereabouts which revealed a surprising discovery: Layla, was no longer at the front door, she was sitting in front of my food cupboard, munching on a packet of my Wotsits that I had bought for my pack-up on Monday. Cheekily, she offered, 'Do you want one?' She was fine and so I went to bed.

The following day, much to our disappointment, Teddy Ruxpin and Rubber Johnny knocked on our door to check in on Layla (so now they gave a shit!) Layla, miraculously recovered, became an unwilling host to Teddy Ruxpin's prolonged visit, as he mysteriously decided to linger like a bad smell for the entire day. Rubber Johnny, however, escaped to fulfil his pub duties, leaving us with Teddy's enduring presence.

Engrossed in the television, Teddy proved oblivious to our subtle hints (not talking to him, and just talking to one another), and Layla and I exchanged eyerolls behind his unsuspecting back.

It became abundantly clear that Teddy Ruxpin had an excessive amount of time on his hands, and I couldn't fathom whether he believed overstaying his welcome was the golden key to Layla's heart.

Lingering resentment from his prior night's antics of leaving us stranded simmered within me, fuelling an internal rage as the day progressed. I was so angry with him.

Getting hungry, I casually offered Layla some toast, only to have Teddy Ruxpin say, 'I'll have some, please.' Firmly dismissing his request, I responded, 'I wasn't asking you.' We then sat there and munched our toast in front of him.

Our house we resided in on Cherry Tree Road in Mill Hill East was quiet and not really what I envisaged London life to be like. Don't get me wrong I always had a wake-up call of the hustle and bustle, pushing and shoving on the underground everyday Monday to Friday and sometimes Mill Hill was a great escape from all this.

Frequently, I organised gatherings, enticing my friends to travel from Market Deeping for a night out. The highlight of my 25th birthday celebration unfolded one night when Layla, along with my friends Kerrie and Grace, embarked on a journey to the glamourous Embassy nightclub in Mayfair. This venue was renowned for hosting celebrities, footballers, and Big-Brother stars. Such glamourous nightclubs always captivated me, though they weren't necessarily Layla's preferred choice. Nevertheless, Kerrie, Grace, and I found excitement in these very walls.

After disembarking from the tube and making our way through the city streets to the nightclub. A fire truck stopped next to us at the traffic lights with their window down. In a jesting manner, I quipped, 'Can we have a lift, please?' To our surprise, a dark-haired and fairly handsome fireman replied, 'Yeah, get in.'

We couldn't believe it! With his assistance, we excitedly all clambered into the back of the fire truck, trying on the firemen's hats and capturing the moment with lots of photos. The prospect of arriving at Embassy in this attention-grabbing vehicle with authentic firemen was beyond thrilling.

My excitement, however, was short-lived as they received an emergency call and promptly shoved us out of the truck just a street away. FFS!

My friend Grace, despite being in a five-year relationship, had an admirable confidence with the opposite sex. She had an ability to charm her way into getting a free drink wherever she went. 'Watch and learn, girls,' she declared, strutting off towards a group of men placing their orders at the bar. She strode up next to the guy conversating with the bar lady and boldly says, 'Mine will be a double-Bacardi and coke, please.'

As we watched eagerly, anticipating his reaction, Grace, faced an unexpected setback. The guy responded, 'No, I know your game.' Layla, Kerrie, and I erupted into laughter as Grace returned to us, with her tail between her legs, wearing a defeated expression.

Layla doing her usual disappearing act on a night out, wasn't to be seen for a while. So, I assumed that she had got chatting to some guy.

I got distracted by her whereabouts as I encountered the most striking 6ft 4 guy, standing alone in the nightclub, who made a beeline for me near the women's toilets.

Introducing himself as Andre, he had an air of seriousness and sensibility about him, and with his dark features and muscular body I was totally up for a quick chat. We engaged in a brief conversation as I was eager to rejoin my friends, but not before exchanging numbers and agreeing to arrange a date.

As I pulled out my phone, I had realised that Layla had tried calling me 14 times.

Feeling a pang of worry, I excused myself and walked away from Andre. I went to the toilets where it was quieter and called Layla. She had been kicked out of Embassy Nightclub for taking off her shoes, cutting her feet and walking around the place drunk with blood-stained toilet tissue wrapped around her feet.

I grabbed the rest of the girls, and we scurried out of the club to find Layla. Luckily, she was waiting outside for us and despite all the blood she wasn't too badly hurt. We decided to call it a night.

Returning home that night, I found a message from Andre and a few days later, we had our first date at a quiet local pub, and it proved surprisingly good fun. He appeared in a brand-new, expensive-looking Range Rover, and the following day, he arrived for coffee in a sleek Mercedes. Andre casually mentioned owning his own business, but amidst our conversations, I never quite found out the specifics.

It wasn't until I began piecing together certain hints and turned to Google that I discovered he was a Queens Park Rangers footballer and was being very secretive about this. Opting not to ask him, our text exchanges and calls eventually dwindled after I wasn't forthcoming responding to his sext messages.

Rick wanted me to chase after Andre, but more so because he was initially drawn to living in London because he wanted to hang out in celebrity hotspots. He saw this as an opportunity to be able to dive into this world.

Rick started hanging around in pubs in Highgate, hoping to rub shoulders with the famous and make some high-profile friends. But after a few unsuccessful attempts—where the closest he got to fame was overhearing a conversation about a local reality show—Rick threw in the towel and instead started returning to his mum's house every weekend.

It wasn't surprising, he was very well looked after; he would come back on the Sunday evening with his sandwiches made for the week, and an evening meal for every day of the week until he went back home to his Mum's every Friday evening after work.

Not as impressed as us with living in London, he missed his mum and home back in Cambridge and Rick eventually declared his intention to move out, prompting

Layla and me to go on yet another search for a new housemate through an advert on Gumtree.

Enter Steve and his girlfriend Madeline, a seemingly lively couple who showed enthusiasm for the room. Steve was working in London and his girlfriend would travel from Liverpool every weekend to spend time together with him.

But despite their initial excitement for the room, once Steve moved in their vibrant energy quickly disappeared and was replaced by Steve's occasional complaints about noise and their tendency to isolate themselves in his room every weekend.

One Thursday evening at 9pm Layla and I were watching a comedy film and laughing away. Steve comes down the stairs in his boxers with his hairy chest on display and shouted at us to turn the TV down. I'm not sure if Layla and I were deaf but it wasn't even loud. We looked at him bewildered, is he being serious? I muttered 'ok, sorry Steve' and we just turned the TV off and looked at each other baffled with 'naughty schoolgirl' smirks on our faces.

As soon as Steve got upstairs and slammed his bedroom door. We burst into giggles trying to be quiet, but it was impossible.

The atmosphere became quite hostile. Steve clearly wasn't impressed with Layla and me.

Despite his fun-killer aura, he came to be useful to me one day. Sort of a hero, in a way.

Being naturally brunette and determined to stay blonde, I searched for a local hairdressing salon to tackle my dark roots. I stumbled upon what seemed like an up-market yet affordable place in Weston Central. Booking an appointment one Saturday afternoon, I was greeted by the most flamboyant hairdresser I'd ever encountered. 'This is going to be fun,' I thought.

We spent hours chatting, swapping stories about men, and giggling away. Finally, my hair was highlighted and dried. As I looked in the mirror, expecting golden locks, I was greeted by... an old lady staring back at me with grey hair! Panic struck me and my heart started pounding. 'Does my hair look grey to you?' I asked nervously.

'No darling, it's ash blonde,' he reassured me.

Relieved, I walked out, smiling and saying I loved it. But as I passed a shop window and looked at my reflection, my heart sank – I still looked like someone's grandma out for a stroll.

Back home in Mill Hill East, I burst into the kitchen where Steve was making a sandwich and Layla was washing up. They weren't conversing because they had absolutely nothing in common. 'Does my hair look grey to you?' I blurted out in distress.

Steve remained silent, while Layla chirped, 'No, it's blonde, Lucy!'

Desperate for a second opinion, I dashed to the hallway mirror. It was unmistakably dyed grey.

'Are you sure?' I pleaded with Layla.

'Definitely blonde, Lucy,' she insisted, perhaps trying to ease my soon-to-be meltdown.

Turning to Steve, I asked, 'What do you see?'

'Grey hair,' he replied.

I fucking knew it.

I then desperately asked Simon for a lift back to the salon (he was the only one with a car at this point) and he gladly agreed, and I was dropped off. I pleaded with my new flamboyant 'friend' to fix my hair before work on Monday. After a heated discussion over his denial of my grandma hair, he reluctantly agreed to fix it the next day.

Sam who had been with us from the beginning of our tenancy was easy going and forever laid back and had an extremely posh accent, he was hardly ever there but when he was, he brought warmth to our home. When he did walk through the front door, he greeted us with his high-energy and enthusiastic signature 'Hey guys' and then would always retreat to his room.

Sam, Layla and I decided to have a night out in Hoxton to get to know Sam better. A well-known DJ that Layla knew of was playing that night. The queue was massive, so Layla and I decided to pretend to the door staff that we were 'press' despite having no press passes or proof of this so we could walk straight in and avoid waiting in the queue.

It worked and the doorman let us in. Layla was buzzing and Sam was enthusiastic before he got hit on the head by a flying glass bottle. Layla's face dropped, was Sam about to ruin her night? She had a look on her face to suggest 'don't make this all about you Sam' and carried on dancing.

I the more concerned one asked him if he was ok. In good spirits he shrugged it off and we carried on the night.

Despite Sam's calm nature, his room was a disaster zone. When he was out, Layla and I couldn't resist occasional giggles at the sight of his bedroom, complete with clothes thrown everywhere, beard shavings and what looked like pubes scattered on the floor, and a stack of mouldy plates piled up in the corner.

Layla and I one drunken night, decided to do him a 'favour' and clean up his room whilst he was out. Armed with a hoover, duster and mop we set to work on transforming the dirty, messy, pube-infested room.

His room looked unrecognisable once we had finished with it. We felt really proud of ourselves and in our tipsy state was convinced he would be over the moon arriving home to such cleanliness and now an organised looking sanctuary for him.

Sam's new clean room was never mentioned by him, and he carried on being his friendly self to us. I'm not sure who was more embarrassed sober Layla and I, or Sam.

He later only bothered cleaning his room when he started dating a new girl and bringing her home. When he was out, we would continue to open the door of his room and poke our heads in to see if he had kept on top of his cleanliness. We were impressed but slightly gutted that this was the end of our giggles being able to look at a room so filthy.

At this point in my London journey, I had befriended a peculiar character named Kay. Meeting him at Embassy nightclub, I found him to be a supposed wealthy man, but secretive, and I was unsure of his intentions and not knowing what he did for a living. But I had a suspicion that it was something dodgy.

Kay often dropped by for a cup of tea and Layla enjoyed his chat too, cos he was one of those guys who just chatted absolute bullshit, that you knew all the tales he was telling were never true. Yet, we found him amusing and entertaining because of this.

However, our friendship reached an abrupt end when he suggested that I lose weight to fit into a size 6, promising an expensive designer dress as a reward. Outraged, I dismissed the idea, cherishing my size 10-12 body and self-respect. What a knob.

Shortly afterwards, I encountered Charles, an adorable French guy, during a night out on Oxford Street with Layla.

We got chatting near a bus stop after someone from a flat above chucked a lit cigarette butt out of the window onto the street and it landed on top of his friend's head.

Charles and I spent a few months together, during which he proved caring, kind, and humorous.

He would speak to my Mum on the phone and speak French, which my mum is fluent in. He would have fitted into our family very well.

But, despite his perfection, I didn't make the time for him that he deserved, which he wasn't happy about. I felt the need to prioritize my social life that London offered, and we parted ways.

Layla had been spending a lot of time at Bar Vinyl in Camden with her friend Greg, who lived above the bar, adding a lively atmosphere for her away from the quiet place of Mill Hill East.

The desire for a more vibrant London experience led Layla to suggest that her and I move to Stoke Newington. Intrigued by her enthusiasm, I agreed, and Layla took charge of flat hunting in Stokey whilst I embarked on a trip to Las Vegas with Kerrie and our friends Lisa and Emily.

I had the time of my life in Las Vegas—pool parties, Cirque du Soleil, breakfast at the Bellagio, and staying at the MGM Grand. It was surreal seeing a real lion in an enclosure at the hotel, which we walked past every day. I kept having visions of it escaping at night and eating me in my sleep.

We took photos outside the famous 'Welcome to Las Vegas, Nevada' sign and even visited the Little White Wedding Chapel where Britney got married.

We flew to the Grand Canyon in a small 8-seater plane, and poor Kerrie got flight sick because it was so rocky up in the air. Visiting the Grand Canyon was one of the best experiences of my life. Whilst there, we met real-life Native Americans, tribal members who lived in the Canyon. It was a world away from the streets of London.

During the day, we sunbathed, and I read a book called 'How to Get from Where You Want to Be' by Jack Canfield. I kept peering over my book at all the super-hot six-packs in the pool, it was a beautiful scenery to be in. It was the first motivational book I had ever read, and I was hooked. I had this surge of energy that I was going to change my life after this book and live a life full of experiences like being in Las Vegas on a regular basis.

Back in Mill Hill East, after not sleeping on the 9-hour flight and partying hard in Vegas, I ended up with a really bad case of tonsillitis. Despite feeling awful, I knew I had a week of flat hunting with Layla, who had been searching for us while I was away.

After Vegas it spurred me on even more that I would like to live in a livelier and more vibrant environment. Despite Mill Hill East's tranquil and quieter setting, we created cherished memories, with one standout being what we fondly dubbed 'Snow-Day' in December 2008. A heavy snowfall led to the cancellation of buses and tubes, granting us a day off work. Get in!

Layla and I seized the opportunity, purchasing wine, bacon, and bread rolls from the local garage. We spent the day indoors, watching old films, indulging in bacon rolls, and getting pissed as farts and completely relishing the unexpected day of relaxation.

Yet, even in Stoke Newington, we envisioned a similar scenario—same sofa, same rules, and the absence of other housemates, promising blissful moments closer to the heart of London.

Chapter Ten

Flat Hunting and Pub Brawls: Settling into Stoke Newington

LAYLA

Whilst Lucy was 'living-it-up' in the dazzling lights of Las Vegas, I was back in the damp streets of London, and on a quest for our next home. My heart led us to the vibrant neighbourhoods of Hackney and Stoke Newington, where my journey had originally begun.

Stoke Newington, a lively place with an eclectic mix of shops, bars, and restaurants, beckoned us with its charm. The only drawback – no tube line. Yet, buses crisscrossed the area, and an overground service connected us to the bustling Liverpool Street station.

Armed with determination and a laptop, I embarked on the modern-day house hunt, scouring local ads on Gumtree during stolen moments of free Wi-Fi at work. A couple of letting agents in Hackney caught my eye, prompting me to make a call. Swiftly, they sent me an email, attached to which was a long list of available rentals.

As soon as Lucy returned from her holiday, we eagerly scheduled viewings for potential homes, narrowing down our choices from a lengthy list of more than twenty options, we miraculously spotted two options that didn't laugh in the face of our budget. Meeting on the bustling Oxford Street after a day's work, we embarked on our adventure with excitement.

The first property, we were told and having done no research, was situated atop Church Street in Stoke Newington and it seemed like it could be promising.

We greeted the lettings agent at the top of Church Street. But hold on to your moving boxes because the lettings agent had a little surprise for us – our dream pad was just a short drive away from where he asked us to meet him.

He said that he would take us in his car, we both looked at each other, unsure if this was a safe and sensible thing to do, but ultimately we went along with it, pushing any thoughts of danger to the back of our minds.

Well, it was not exactly worth the risk of potentially being kidnapped and murdered by a serial killer posing as a cheap London lettings agent. The windows were covered with bars! NEXT!

The lettings agent dropped us back onto Church Street and we made our own way to the second flat, on Stoke Newington High Street, it was above the local Sainsbury's. This one looked more promising—who wouldn't want the ultimate convenience of having a grocery store (and off-licence) on their doorstep?

Three flights of grimy and gloomy stairs later, we reached the top of the building.

We knocked and waited. No answer. We knocked again. Nobody was coming.

Hmm. I start to dial the number of the agent when a couple of guys came bounding up the stairs.

They introduced themselves, and we established that they were the owners, who then proceeded to show us inside.

Well, this was more like it! Not exactly the Ritz, but it was clean, compact, and the bedrooms were a decent size.

The guy told us that he needed an answer straight away, as he had several people interested. I was sold. I didn't think we were going to find better for our budget, and location-wise, it was perfect. Lucy, on the other hand—always the more cautious and sensible of the two of us—whispered to me that she thought we should haggle for the price.

With Lucy working in buying and negotiating with jewellery suppliers on a daily basis, she seemed to think she had top-notch negotiation skills.

If Lucy was ever in a hostage situation, she'd be the one standing up, saying, 'Alright, everyone, no need to panic, I've watched *Taken* like, five times—I know what I'm doing.' She'd start negotiating with the kidnapper like she was haggling at a car boot.

God loves a trier, I suppose.

I could tell straight off by looking at the potential landlord that he was NOT in the habit of negotiating with a couple of inexperienced twenty-something girls from the sticks. Still, I humoured her and let her do 'her thing.'

With a serious look on her face, Lucy ventured, 'We really like the place, but it's a matter of the price. Our maximum is 500 pounds a month.'

The owner cuts her off with a dose of reality: 'No negotiations, love. It's 550 each a month—take it or leave it.'

Lucy, with a resigned 'okay,' gave up quickly, leaving me to ponder how she ended up with a career in buying that required negotiating costs with suppliers on the daily. But hey ho.

Four weeks later, we found ourselves settling into our new place in Stoke Newington—I'll skip the dull moving stuff. But first, let's flash back to our last day at Mill Hill East. Sam and Steve were smart enough to move out the day before, leaving Lucy and me to clean the flat with help from Lucy's mum. After the place was spotless, we all pitched in to load up the van Lucy's dad had hired, packed full of our furniture and endless boxes of stuff.

I had just one task left: lock the door before we set off. Simple, right? As we drove away, Lucy's dad cheerfully said, 'Goodbye Mill Hill East!' We all turned for one last sentimental look at the house... only to see I'd done a fantastic job—by leaving the front door wide open! One job, and I practically invited the whole neighbourhood to move in right after us!

I'll spare you the rest of the mundane moving details. Instead let's dive into the exciting part: our first night out in Stoke Newington!

Thrilled to be back living on the doorstep of a vibrant London suburb filled with pubs and bars, we embarked on a Friday night adventure, ready to explore and, inevitably, get a bit messy.

As we walked down the high street, we stumbled upon a lively pub with bass-heavy music and a crowd spilling out of its doors. Intrigued, we walked in, ordered drinks, and carved out a space in the midst of the chaos.

It didn't take long for us to realize that, amidst the lively atmosphere, there were quite a few sketchy characters lingering around. A couple of drinks deep, inhibitions tossed out the window, we slipped into our usual routine – chatting with strangers and discreetly scoping out potential romantic interests.

However, our routine came to an abrupt halt when a commotion erupted on the other side of the pub. A full-blown fight had broken out, with glass bottles flying and the dance area transformed into a chaotic battleground.

We were excited by the sudden injection of drama, but we wisely decided to make a swift exit, finding ourselves outside contemplating the next place to go.

Eavesdropping on a conversation amongst a group of guys, they noticed us and strolled over to strike up a chat.

The scent of weed caught my attention, and in my drunken state, I found myself impulsively inviting myself to one of the guy's houses for a smoke session.

Lucy, exercising her better judgment, opted to head home. The tall, smoulderingly attractive man amongst the group offered to escort Lucy home. At 6ft 4 and with undeniable good looks Lucy was more than content with the arrangement as we went our separate ways into the night.

I found myself sharing a taxi with weed man and his friends, heading back to his place. The irony hung thick in the air – this guy actually lived in the projects on the very same estate of the place we viewed with bars, the one we were completely horrified by.

But before I knew it, I was perched in a room with the presence of drug dealers and a pit bull terrier as my companions, the reality of my choices began to sober me up.

As the smell of a shared spliff wafted through the room, I couldn't escape the realization that this venture might not have been amongst my most brilliant decisions.

The tipping point arrived in the form of the massive pit bull terrier leaving a big dump in the middle of the living room floor. I desperately attempted to call a taxi, only to be met with the harsh reality that dawn had already broken. The birds were cheeping, and faced with limited options, my only option was an early morning stroll home.

Unbeknown to me, whilst all this was going on, Lucy had in fact invited Mr 6.4 up for a cup of tea, and when I say a cup of tea, this is not a euphemism, she really would have meant just a cup of tea. I can only imagine his disappointment.

She later told me, she had a lovely chat with Mr 6ft.4 over their cups of tea, she had casually asked about his occupation. An essential question in Lucy's world, only to be met with the revelation that he had been spending time at Her Majesty's pleasure.

Lucy, ever the inquisitive soul, couldn't contain her excitement and blurted out, 'Ooh, lucky you! Did you get to meet the queen?'

He had to politely explain that he wasn't there working with the queen; in fact, he had just gotten out of prison. Lucy, being naturally curious and non-judgemental, sympathetically enquired about the circumstances that led him there. His response was armed robbery.

By the time I returned to the flat, reeking of weed, Lucy was already fast asleep, and Mr. 6ft 4 had departed, leaving our belongings in his wake.

Lucy had recently decided to buy herself a nippy little car to get us around more places in London. So, the next morning, with no food in the flat and feeling hungover, hungry and craving carbs, we decided to head out in Lucy's little beast of a Ford KA car to Walthamstow shopping centre where there is an Asda.

Once we parked up, we spotted the shopping trollies in the car park. We popped our pounds in and in ignorance bliss, we headed off to do our food shop.

Upon entering the precinct, we couldn't find Asda, so we carried on walking through the busy shopping centre.

Surrounded by a crowd of busy shoppers, we started to notice that we were the only ones with big heavy duty shopping trollies, suddenly there was a loud 'CLICK' and we both came to an abrupt halt.

Unable to move any further we looked down and to our horror, the wheels had locked.

Unsure what to do at this point, we looked at each other, helpless.

Now in hindsight the most obvious thing to do at this point, would have been to abandon them there and then, but not us, instead we went for option B, which was to drag them backwards through the busy shopping centre, huffing and puffing, faces red with embarrassment but in hysterical fits of giggles. Fellow shoppers were sniggering at us, and we had to laugh along with them to save face.

After what felt like a trek through the Andes, we made it through the golden gates of Asda after realising we had taken the wrong entrance to get there.

The most ridiculous ending to this story is, after all that effort to get there, we changed our minds and dumped the trollies by the doors, heading off in search of Burger King.

The following Saturday morning and in need of shopping Lucy decided to venture to Morrisons in Stamford Hill for the first time. She returned looking a bit puzzled, but with a hint of excitement in her eyes.

'There's a big production going on in Stamford Hill,' she said, setting down her shopping bags. 'Lots of people walking along the streets in fancy dress.'

I raised an eyebrow, curious. 'Oh, what were they wearing?'

'The men all had black hats on with locks of hair falling either side of the hat and all had black outfits on,' she replied earnestly.

I burst out laughing, unable to contain myself. 'Lucy, they're ultra-Orthodox Jews.'

Her eyes widened in realization, and a blush crept up her cheeks. 'Oh... I didn't realize. I thought it was some kind of theatre production or something.'

Her naivety was endearing, and I couldn't help but smile at her innocence. Stamford Hill is known for its large Orthodox Jewish community and seeing them dressed in their traditional attire is a common sight for those familiar with the area. For Lucy, it was a new and surprising discovery.

We spent the rest of the afternoon laughing about the mix-up. Lucy's innocent mistake turned into a learning moment for her and was a reminder of the brilliant diversity of the city we lived in. But fuck me, Lucy must have been living under a rock her whole life.

The next morning, my parents came to visit to have a walk around Hampstead Heath with me. I had met a guy named Mark on one of my drunken nights out, and we had a date planned for late afternoon on the same day. I decided I could fit in all plans and since it was a Sunday, we agreed to just have a couple of drinks. Knowing that I wouldn't be long, my parents decided to stay in London until my date was over so we could have dinner together afterwards.

After a beautiful walk in Hampstead Heath and a good catch-up with my parents, I took the tube to meet Mark in Golders Green. He said he would pick me up down a side street from the station and we would drive to a nearby pub. 'Ok, this looks promising,' I thought.

Standing on the side street, I heard a car horn beep. 'It's him, no time to be nervous now,' I thought. I walked over and pulled open the passenger car door. He looked a bit scruffier than when I first met him, but he seemed 'ok,' worth a drink still.

I climbed into the car, which reeked of weed. With a dirty look on his face, he said, 'You look nice.' I thanked him and shuffled into my seat. I asked, 'So, what pub are we going to?' He replied, 'I thought we could go to McDonald's and smoke some weed instead?'

I politely said, 'No, that's not my idea of a date.' Mark huffed and said, 'Fine, we'll go for a drink as planned.'

We pulled up at the pub and walked in. The place was quiet, but that suited me. Given how the date had started, I wasn't sure how it was going to pan out. We went to the bar and ordered drinks. Whilst the bartender was making our two Bacardi and Cokes, I told him that I needed the toilet. So, off I went to freshen up my hair and makeup. When I came out, Mark was nowhere to be seen.

'Maybe he has gone to the toilet?' I wondered. The bar lady looked at me sympathetically, handed me my drink, and said, 'This one's on the house.' I was mortified. I knew straight away what had happened at this point. No one had ever run out on a date with me before. He'd ordered my drink, then left without paying.

So, I sat and chatted with the bar lady, having a couple more drinks on the house. The highlight of this date was definitely the free drinks. As I sipped my Bacardi and Coke, I couldn't help but wonder why on earth he ditched me. Did he have a sudden realisation that he doesn't want a girl who doesn't think McDonald's and weed was a great idea for a first date?

I decided to call my dad. 'Dad, my date did a disappearing act on me when I went to the toilets. Can you pick me up? I really don't feel like taking the tube back feeling this wounded.'

'Of course, sweetheart. Your mum and I will ring you when we're at Golders Green and let you know where we are,' he replied.

So, there I was, 27 years old, sitting at a bar, waiting for my mum and dad to pick me up after my date did a runner. If this wasn't a low point, I didn't know what was.

The bar lady, tried to cheer me and said, 'You know, if a guy can't handle a simple drink date, he's not worth your time.'

'True.' I laughed. 'But still, who does that? I can't believe this has happened. I am mortified!'

She laughed and said, 'Well, at least you have had some free drinks, rather than a spliff and a burger!'

Even though I was mortified that my parents had to know about this disastrous date on the night it happened, I'd have hoped to have licked my wounds before having a laugh with them later down the line about it. But them being there was a nice reminder that no matter what they would always come to the rescue.

When I got back to the flat and after my parents had driven home. I started to tell Lucy about the date that did the magic disappearing act. Aswell as my parents she made me see the funny side of it, and with my spirits a little higher, we decided to pop down to Saino's and grab some wine and Monster Munch. I drank way too much, probably drowning my sorrows from the terrible date. Whose idea was it to get so smashed on a Sunday evening?

The next morning, I felt ill and as I was making my way to work on the daily commute, I had to crawl off at Euston station because I felt like I was going to pass out.

The truth was, I was completely hungover and thought, 'If I don't get off soon, I'm going to throw up on the person standing next to me.' It was minutes, if not seconds, from happening.

What I hadn't bargained on was my boss coming and standing over me while I was slumped in a crumpled mess on the side of the platform. She was always traveling to meetings on the tube. It was just my bad luck that we crossed paths that day.

I'm not sure she bought my story about a sudden sickness bug, but she humoured me and pretended to show sympathy. She went off on her travels, and I, mortified, reluctantly got back on the tube and made my way to work. It was not a good day. I spent most of it in the staff toilets, throwing up and taking two-minute power naps.

Chapter Eleven

Blame It on the Cardigan

LUCY

One Saturday night, after an evening out at Kimo's—the RnB haven in Stokey—with Kerrie and Layla, I stumbled out of the bar. As, I tried to steady myself, a tall, dark, and handsome man walked by, locking eyes with me and giving a cheeky wink. My only thought? 'Corrrrrr, he's a bit of alright.'

An internal debate went off in my head – was he flirting with me? Or did he have an eye-twitch? Alcohol consumption could be blurring my instinct.

As he walked off, he turned back and winked again. I realised at this point, that it probably was intentional.

Regardless, the need to explore this intriguing encounter surged within me after having no potential dates on the horizon and not knowing if I would ever see him again.

After a quick chat with Kerrie about my new crush and with new-found determination, Kerrie, armed with her 5ft 1 frame, sprinted up Stoke Newington High Street waving a napkin in the air with my number on (I moved to the outside of a taxi office spying out of the doorway and hoping that I wasn't in view of his sight). I observed her catch up with him and saw her slipping the napkin into his hand.

As I anxiously awaited her return, the mysterious expression on Kerrie's face as she was walking back towards me divulged nothing as to how this went down.

Winksalot was gradually fading from view, leaving me in suspense. The uncertainty hung in the air, and I couldn't help but daydream that he could be 'the one' and what a great story it would be to tell our Grandkids.

Chasing a man down the street worked! He took my number off the napkin, messaged me and we agreed to meet the following evening at The Wagon and Horses, a pub that was a stone's throw away from mine and Layla's flat. In a deliberate attempt to look 'cute' I opted for a green floral mini dress, complimented by black tights,

Mary-jane heels and topped this with my trusty black leather jacket.

The next evening as I walked down Stoke Newington High Street, I saw my handsome date coming towards me. He was wheeling something next to him. This cannot be. He had a PUSH BIKE with him!

Oh, sweet Jesus. The date hadn't even started yet, this was NOT a good sign. I mean I'm no snob. I like a good bike ride on a summer's day, but this was pushing it too far (no pun intended).

This was not the romantic first date that I had pictured in my head. I didn't expect him to come riding along on a white horse, but what was he going to do give me a backy home?

'This part of the story won't be in our wedding speech,' I thought.

'Hey, babe,' Winksalot says as we are now face to face. He had the deepest, sexiest voice and he leaned in for a greeting kiss on my cheek. Without delay, we made our way inside the Wagon and Horses pub where Amani (which we will call him now from here on in) confidently ordered a whiskey, and I opted for a red wine Shiraz.

Settling into our seats, the conversation flowed effortlessly. He delved into conversation about his music career, proudly wearing the hat of an MC in the vibrant scene of East London. At 32 years old, he was a touch older than me at 25 years old, and in that moment, it struck me –

this man given his age must have his shit together, despite turning up to a first date on a push bike. I was wondering if he could give me some tips.

The date was going really well, and I extended an invitation for Amani to join me back at mine and Layla's flat for a civilized cup of tea. Not wanting the night to end.

We stepped into the flat and settled around the 4-seater table, engrossed in conversation. Layla, returned from her night out with a hint of tipsiness, joined us and introduced herself to Amani.

She stood behind one of the vacant dining chairs. Layla was looking utterly cool as she leant on the chair with a laidback air about her (I knew that she had this chilled, confident vibe going on because she was drunk, but Amani probably didn't have a clue).

As the chatter continued, Layla noticed a cardigan slipping off the back of the chair that she was leaning on, prompting her to bend down swiftly to retrieve it.

However, in a surprising turn of events, an unmistakable FRRRRPPPPPPP resonated from her rear-end as she bent down. She shot back up, holding the cardigan up in disgust and was angrily staring at it (I didn't know cardigans could fart).

Much like the fart she lingered, frozen in time and working out her next move.

How could she come back from this?

I just wanted to fall on the floor laughing, but to not be disrespectful and embarrass her further I inwardly laughed with my shoulders moving up and down.

I looked at Amani with a big smirk on my face, but Amani looked shocked to the core. He didn't find it even remotely amusing. Much to my disappointment cos I really needed someone to laugh with about it in that moment. I didn't know how much longer I could keep the laughter in. I found it so amusing, it was hurting.

Layla scurried out of the room a shade of awkwardness, and Amani looked on after her with a pitiful look. She didn't say a word and didn't even stifle a giggle. I mean, she could have helped me out. She was the one that farted, and she had left me to try and explain her uncontrollable bowel movements.

Soon after, Amani leaves, and I couldn't wait for his exit. All I wanted to do was open Layla's bedroom door, point at her, and let out a hearty laugh as loud as her fart.

I never heard from Amani again. In hindsight, it was for the best. It was evident that we didn't share the same sense of humour.

The following weekend I found myself on a night out in Richmond, Surrey, with my work colleague Ellie and her friends.

The night was good fun, it involved a visit to a bar where a reasonably good-looking guy approached, offering to buy me a drink.

I didn't feel any chemistry because his personality was a bit stiff, so I politely declined, stating that I already had a drink. Despite my refusal, he persisted, disappearing momentarily only to return with a drink in hand for me.

Our conversation unfolded, and as the night went on and being in my slightly tipsy state of adoring everyone, we exchanged numbers. Although I wasn't overly impressed with his personality, he was a pharmacist so I thought that he must be clever, and he appeared seemingly 'normal' so I thought 'perhaps he could be interesting.'

We arranged a date.

The following Monday after work I arrived to meet him at a bar in Islington. Anticipation hung in the air, heightened by the absence of zero familiar faces.

With a huff in my thoughts that he was late, I went straight to the bar to grab a drink. At the bar, a tall, dark-haired gentleman with glasses catches my eye. He seemed oddly familiar, but it couldn't have been him because with only standing a few people's width away, he gazed in my direction without uttering a word. My memory was still a bit hazy from the weekend.

Scepticism lingered – 'Could it be him? No, of course not; he hasn't said anything.'

Nevertheless, I proceeded to order my drink.

To my surprise, after I got my drink in my hand the tall, dark-haired guy with glasses broke the silence in a casual and creepy sounding quiet voice 'hello, Lucy.'

A revelation washed over me; he was there all along. A subtle sense of discomfort settled in, but I decided to stay for the drink, nonetheless. The encounter didn't shock me that after the weird start to the date Mr Pharmacist proved to be more boring, weird, and creepy than anticipated.

I was carrying most of the conversation whilst he stared at me with the kind of intensity that screamed, 'I have a freezer full of mystery meat back at home.' The guy had serious serial killer in disguise vibes.

I made up some excuse, slid out of that weird date, and as I walked away, I couldn't help but wonder just how much I had to drink in Richmond to end up on a date with this walking true crime special.

I got back to the flat with a text from Mr Pharmacist asking when we can do it again. I messaged back thanking him for the date but mentioned that I thought we had very different personalities and I wouldn't want to waste his time by going on a second date.

Meeting a 'normal' guy in London was becoming quite a challenge. I was ready to give up.

The following Thursday, I decided to meet up with Rick, even though he no longer lived with us; he was commuting from Cambridge to London still for work. We opted for a bar in Islington, taking advantage of the warm weather by choosing to sit outside a lovely, cosmopolitan, plush bar on the main strip.

Ordering glasses of wine, I noticed the bouncer standing outside and frequently glancing in my direction. He had kind eyes and was just 'my type'. However, he seemed a bit too young, likely around 21, while I, at 25, considered myself much more mature.

Not interested, I focused on my evening with Rick.

As we sat chatting, a homeless man approached, asking if we had any spare change. He explained that he was sleeping in the park nearby and needed money for a room in a shelter for the night. In my overly confident, tipsy state, I politely enquired, 'Can I ask what led you to the streets?'

He shared that he had a wife and hailed from Blackpool, but his wife kicked him out and he had nowhere to go, so he moved to London with no place to stay. Approximately 40 years old at the time, he captivated us with his story. I invited him to join us, and as Rick went to the bar and bought him a drink, the homeless man expressed a simple wish: to wash his hands but the bar had refused him entry.

My heart ached for him, realizing that everyday privileges we take for granted were denied to him due to circumstances beyond his control.

Driven by empathy, I approached the bouncer who had taken a shine to me, explaining the situation. To my relief, he agreed to let the homeless man enter through a back door, personally escorting him to the toilets for a much-needed hand wash. Hallelujah.

The homeless man rejoined Rick and me, his hands now appearing refreshed, and the bouncer strolled by, offering a wink in my direction after I thanked him. Perhaps the age difference wasn't a problem after all; what a sweetheart. Rick and I would get a drink for the homeless man every time we got one for us, and we sat chatting to him for hours.

Rick needed to head back and get his train so before we left, I enquired about the homeless man's needs.

He explained, 'It's too late for me to go into a shelter now, but just a packet of cigarettes and two litres of cider will keep me warm until I get to the shelter tomorrow.' Apologetically, I felt responsible for keeping him from a warm place for the night.

Hovering on the brink of inviting him back to mine and Layla's flat, I chose instead to inform Rick that I would return in a moment. I headed to the local Tesco, procured the cider and cigarettes, and withdrew £20 – an expense I couldn't really afford, but let's face it, I was far better off than him; I had a roof over my head.

The homeless man assured me that this would be his last night on the streets. Sadly, it wasn't. Every time, that I took the 73-bus, and it passed by the park where he slept, I spotted him there without fail with a bottle of cider in his hand.

I wondered whether he would remember me, our conversation, and the goals that he set himself to get off the streets. Despite returning to a small flat, I felt grateful to be warm and safe and I understood that it must have been very hard for him and of course, I didn't really know what obstacles he was up against other than what he told me.

I did, however, exchange numbers with the bouncer. We engaged in some text conversations, but his messages were laden with street slang. We met for a single drink the following week, and although he appeared to have a heart of gold, I found myself unable to understand half of the street' slang that he spoke. Consequently, our connection couldn't progress any further.

After this…I met a guy on the tube. Noticing his untied shoelace, I offered a casual observation. To be honest, I did find him rather attractive; after all, I wouldn't have gone around informing just anyone about their undone shoelaces.

Taking my comment as an invitation, he swopped seats and came to sit next to me on the tube. We got off the tube and had a couple of drinks in Islington.

After the drinks, we decided to share a taxi, and it would drop me home first. However, when we reached Stoke Newington High Street, bid our farewells in the taxi, and I stepped out of the taxi, I was startled to find him stepping out of the taxi as well.

Shocked I asked him about his unexpected departure, only to learn he was hoping for an invitation inside. I politely told him to fuck off.

He was only after one-thing, and I was so annoyed that he had assumed I would be game.

Then there was 'bus man'... On the scorching 73 bus back from work during the height of summer, I found myself surrounded by an overpowering scent of BO. Amidst the discomfort, a dark-haired guy with captivating eyes, who was slightly shorter than average was trying to catch my eye. I returned the glance with a smile, appreciating the face that met my gaze.

The glances back and forth intensified as he got off the bus at Church Street, just around the corner from our high-street flat. As the bus doors closed, he silently mouthed, 'get off at the next stop.'

'How romantic,' I thought, envisioning a scene straight out of a film.

Nervous but intrigued, I decided to play along. The possibility of a grand love story unfolded before me. Imagining my blonde hair blowing with the opening of the bus doors and intensely looking at one another with a deep chemistry and embracing one another as soon as I stepped off the bus.

Anyway, I got off at the next stop, and he approached with a familiar connection between us. Not quite the chemistry I had imagined but the random meet-up wasn't awkward considering.

We took a stroll in Clissold Park, conversation flowed effortlessly. But then, he suggested, 'Do you want to come back to my basement? I have a photography studio in there, but we can chill and have some drinks.'

Alarm bells rang, and visions of horror movies flooded my mind. Politely declining, I swapped numbers, but his silence echoed loud, and I never saw him on the 73 bus ever again.

Chapter Twelve

Gingerbread Man

LAYLA

Since I had moved back to Stoke Newington, instead of always taking the 73 bus to work, we also had the option to catch the 106 bus to Finsbury Park tube station. From there, we could hop onto the Victoria Line and head straight to Oxford Street.

This particular morning, we took this route, we were packed into the tube like sardines, squashed against the doors. The tube stopped at Euston Station. As usual, a wave of people spilled out onto the platform, and another wave surged in.

Suddenly, as the doors were about to close, a 6'5' giant appeared out of nowhere and launched himself towards the tube. He managed to get himself on, but as the door slammed shut his backpack was left hanging outside of the doors, still attached to his back!

Everyone on the tube stared at him, including us. This being London, no one wanted to get involved.

The man frantically bashed the button to open the doors and retrieve his bag, desperate to get it back before the tube sped off into the tunnel with his backpack flapping away.

Lucy and I could hardly contain ourselves.

We turned away from each other to avoid bursting into fits of giggles.

After what felt like minutes but it was probably only seconds, the doors opened, and the man pulled his bag back inside.

For us, it was a highlight of an otherwise dreary morning commute. For him, it was likely one of the most embarrassing moments of his life.

That evening, after wrapping up after another exhausting day at work. My evening route would sometimes consist of me getting the tube to Islington and I would take a brisk walk from Islington back home after work, which I typically relied on to get my exercise in. But this particular day I decided to take the 73 bus all the way to the flat because I simply couldn't be bothered.

I arrived home before Lucy, so I preheated the oven for the cod cakes and put the peas on the hob. We decided to cut back on our food expenses since we spent so much on going out.

It pained us to walk past Whole Foods every day and see people smugly walking out with their woven bags filled with organic goods. Instead, we mostly shopped at Iceland, where it was £1 for a bag of 10 cod cakes and another £1 for a bag of peas. That was our dinner five days a week. Not counting the wine or our late-night Monster Munch runs that we had in our PJs most nights of the week. It was a bit embarrassing, but we were also 1% proud that the late-night Sainsbury's staff knew us by our first names.

I was sitting on the couch, watching re-runs of *Sex and the City*. Since we didn't have an aerial, the only thing we ever watched was Lucy's DVD set of the series. We bloody loved it though. We related to all the men drama and the highs and lows of living in a big city, even if it was London and not New York.

Chilled out and snuggled on the sofa, I heard a knock at the flat door—unusual, because we never got unexpected visitors. I opened the door to find a rather scruffy man standing there, claiming to be a tenant from one of the flats downstairs. I'd never seen him in my life, but I didn't question him because we never bumped into our neighbours on own floor.

He explained that he was in a bit of a pickle with a delivery and needed a tenner because the driver wouldn't wait for him to go to the cash point. He promised he would return in five minutes to pay me back. I didn't think to challenge him about the cashpoint being downstairs next to Sainsburys. The very door that the 'delivery man' would be walking out of.

Caught off guard, I was more than happy to help. It was rare that I had notes on me, but it was his lucky day, because I only had a £20 note. So, to help a 'neighbour' out, I handed it over. And, in a flash he left and didn't return.

A while later, I heard the door slam open as Lucy burst through the flat door and before I could tell her about my generosity she blurted out, 'Laylaaaaaa, I have an idea!'

I thought, 'Oh, FFS, what idea has she got going on now? A cabbage soup diet for us both again, maybe?' Last time she tried that, our flat stank for weeks, and she lasted two days before tucking into some chicken from Dixy Chicken across the road. It didn't take me long to join her—like 5 seconds, if that.

'Let's try online dating!' she exclaimed.

'Are you kidding me?' I replied, looking at her in disbelief.

She looked almost baffled at my reaction, as if we were behind the times. 'Layla, you'll never guess what. Ellie, who I work with, met her bloke on Plenty of Fish, and now they're moving in together. I didn't realize how they met until she told me today.'

I was hesitant... I didn't know if internet dating was my sort of thing. But much like the Dixy Chicken moment, it didn't take me long to be convinced.

'Okay, let's do this,' I reluctantly said.

The cursor blinked on the empty screen on my laptop. I took a deep breath, my fingers hovering over the keyboard, and finally, with a very hesitant click, I opened the online dating website. It was like stepping into the unknown, but yet a step towards meeting someone rather than just in a bar or a pub. I was covering all options.

Putting together my online dating profile felt weird to expose myself to a world of strangers in the hope of meeting someone. It was before the days of Tinder and Hinge, and it felt unnatural. With each word I typed, I wrestled with the fear of rejection and the hope of acceptance. I chose my photos carefully, selecting the ones that I looked my best in.

With my profile completed, I scrolled through the endless profiles of eligible bachelors. Some were intriguing, others uninspiring, and there was an incredible number of men on there holding a picture of a fish with a big grin on their faces proudly holding their prized catch. NEXT.

Lucy and I sat in the living room on our laptops, having a good giggle about some of the profiles. We even got a message off some of the same men, which automatically ruled these men out.

And then, it happened. The next morning, I had a new message in my inbox from someone who looked like 'my type', like a pencil – tall, skinny but with a pointy nose. He even seemed to have a personality.

We swopped numbers after a few messages and for nights on end, we talked into the early hours of the morning, our conversations were light and fun. The only drawback was that he lived in Essex, but it wasn't that far away, so it didn't put me off.

He was keen and suggested that we meet up in person that weekend. So, on a wet Saturday evening we met for drinks in Camden, and I was relieved to find that he was just as attractive in person as he was in his photos.

The cozy pub set the perfect scene for our first meeting and his confidence helped to settle my nerves, almost instantly. The conversation flowed effortlessly, and I was starting to like this guy. His laughter was infectious, and his stories kept me engaged throughout the evening.

He was a really interesting person, and I couldn't wait to see where it would lead.

Since the initial date had gone so well and logistically, he was in Essex and I was in Stokey, we arranged for him to drive up to see me on the following Saturday during the day at 2pm. As it was the cold month of November, we planned to have some drinks before watching some fireworks and then he would sleep over.

Yes, sleep over. Well, I'm not going to insult your intelligence and explain a sleepover between a man and a woman. You get the picture.

Maybe we were jumping the gun a bit (definitely not following the dating rules about meeting up a few times on neutral ground, just in case he was actually an axe murderer or had a fetish like Anthony Hopkins in *Silence of the Lambs*).

The following Saturday arrived quickly.

It was getting late, he was meant to have been at the flat one hour prior, and I hadn't heard anything... hmmm. Then the phone rang. It was him. He was not happy. He had been driving around and around trying to find somewhere to park his car for the night.

Okay, so I had previously explained to him that we lived on a high street above a supermarket and had no parking. I also suggested it was a good idea to check out places to park in advance. There was a lot of residential parking but only for permit holders.

So, I was slightly irritated he had not taken this advice and instead was frantic and annoyed that he couldn't find anywhere to park and there was no hint of an apology for being so late. Eventually, after a lot of swearing and angry huffs and puffs down the phone, he found somewhere to park. Sorted.

'We have lift-off! Good to go, let's get this date started,' I thought.

He turned up at the flat. But instead of greeting me with a smile, his face was as sour as a soggy grape, and he proceeded to moan and moan about the parking 'issue.' GREAT. I knew by now that his was not going to go well, and he was a completely different person to the man I had met only a week ago. So, I pretended to sympathize with him (inwardly snoring) to shut him up from his moaning.

I introduced him to Lucy, who for some unbeknown reason had decided she was going to have a gingerbread man-making session after borrowing a gingerbread cutter from a local bakery. Instead of buying her own gingerbread cutter, she confidently walked into a local bakery and asked the baker if she could borrow their one gingerbread cutter and would return it the following day.

So, there she was proud of herself for saving money on borrowing rather than buying and was happily shaping away in the kitchen.

'Lucy, this is Mike.'

'Oh, hi Mike, nice to meet you,' Lucy replied with a warm smile.

Silence. Err, okay. To fill the awkwardness Lucy asked him if he would like a gingerbread man once they were ready. He looked at her as if she just asked him to clean our bathroom. Who knew a gingerbread man could be so offensive.

Trying to relax the atmosphere, I escorted Mike to sit down on the sofa. Our lounge was open with the kitchen so thankfully Lucy was still present. Hoping to attempt some small talk and bring more energy to the conversation, I invited Lucy back into the conversation.

Well, it seemed that he didn't do small talk. He pretty much ignored everything she said and waffled on about himself and how he was writing a cookery book. Lucy politely asked him what type of cookery book he was writing, and he replied, 'a cookery book.' Awkward. Lucy gave up asking him anymore questions.

I was seething, absolutely seething. I didn't want him there anymore. I just wanted him to go. I checked out.

Then he finally started talking and introduced us to his 'bed in a bag.' Bed in a fucking what now??? He had brought his own bloody bed! If I had a dick, it would be limp.

The man I fancied on date one had become un-fanciable from the moment he stepped in the door, and then he had brought a bed-in-a-bag, I could no longer take this man seriously.

At this point, I couldn't even look at Lucy. I just knew if I did, we would have both lost it and collapsed on the floor in fits of giggles. I glanced out of the corner of my eye. She had her back to me whilst wiping down the kitchen tops, but her shoulders were going frantically up and down.

I wanted to burst out laughing like a naughty schoolgirl trying not to laugh in class. May I add he also brought along a pink toothbrush.

I knew that this was going to be a long date having an afternoon of drinking and then the awkward travelling together to get to Alexandra Palace Fireworks Festival.

We got to the pub and conversation was painfully awkward, filled with long silences. We were both knocking back the drinks, I was hoping this would help to loosen him up. That didn't work, and so we headed to Alexandra Palace.

With the beautiful fireworks display, I hoped it might eventually spark some personality in Gingerbread man, but still nope. Any conversation that did happen was dry and pretentious, filled with him continuously talking about his cooking book and giving me facts about nutrition. It was like being stuck with a walking Wikipedia page, only less interesting.

Gingerbread man did talk about an upcoming holiday. With fake enthusiasm, I said, 'Oh really, that sounds lovely.'

With a disgusted look on his face, he replied, 'You're not coming.'

Shocked, I replied, 'I didn't ask to come on your holiday.'

With a very serious tone, he said, 'Good, because it's a family holiday.'

At this point, I wished I could have brought along his bed in a bag, but for me, so I could sleep through his weird and boring conversations.

We boarded the bus back to Stoke Newington. I did not want him staying over, but as we had some drinks earlier, he was over the limit to be able to drive home and I couldn't exactly turf him out to sleep in his car. 'Thank heavens for his bed-in-a-bag; at least he wouldn't be sleeping in my bed. He is not welcome,' I thought.

When we got back through the flat doors, I said goodnight and headed straight to bed after tossing his bed-in-a-bag in the lounge for him to sleep on. I shut my door and went to sleep wanting to put this horrible night behind me.

Upon waking the next morning, I cautiously and quietly tip-toed out of my room bracing myself for an awkward conversation with Gingerbread man. But, to my surprise and luck, he had already left with his bed-in-a-bag, pink toothbrush and moody personality. Thank fuck.

Unsurprisingly, I never heard from him again. It probably wouldn't have mattered anyway. His pretentious demeanour would likely have clashed with my humble dinners of cod cakes and peas, and I wasn't going to change my budget week-night dinners for him.

Luckily, I had a night out with Lucy and her friends to look forward to the following weekend, I knew that this would take my mind off of bed-in-a-bag man. We decided to go to Coco club in Camden. We had a brilliant night, all dressed up and danced out.

We headed back to the flat and in my drunken state, I decided it was the perfect time to showcase my yoga moves in the front room. Standing on my head, downward dog, sun salutation—the whole shebang.

Lucy looked like she was about to piss herself at me taking my yoga so seriously, whilst her friends just looked a bit shocked. In my drunken state I was very sure it was because they were impressed, and I carried on.

But then, around the third downward dog, I let out a massive FRRRRRPPPP from my backside. For fuck's sake. In a quick flash of thought I wondered if they heard me.

Oh no, they did. Lucy burst out laughing, followed by her friends in hysterics. I didn't get away with it, so I joined in the laughter, trying to save face. I needed an excuse for my surprise fart, so I blurted out, 'Oh, it's the aloe vera I'm taking.'

They all burst out laughing even harder. From that day forward, Lucy sometimes greeted me with 'alooooo Vera,' because it sounded like 'hello Vera,' and we both knew what she was really referring to.

It seemed like people in my life loved using metaphors for breaking wind. When I was recounting my embarrassing story to my mum over the phone, she couldn't help but laugh. Then she said, 'Oh, Layla, I can't believe you pulled a 'Dirty Donald' (Trump).

Chapter Thirteen

The Elephants Upstairs

LUCY

I was thrilled when Layla agreed to join Plenty of Fish with me. I didn't want to do something like that alone, and we were having such a great time setting up our profiles over wine. It felt strange to put ourselves out there for the world to see, but there we were, doing our thing and contributing to the society of singletons.

My online dating profile:

Lucy – *25 years old, enjoys cooking, country walks, going to the gym and healthy eating. Kind-hearted with a great sense of humour. Looking for someone who doesn't take themselves too seriously and enjoys a good giggle. I'm*

5ft 3 and blonde. If you think we'll get on, send me a message and let's date.

Cringe, but simple. When it comes to online dating and setting up a profile to attract some eligible bachelors, telling a few white lies is okay, right? So, I hadn't been country walking in three years, but Layla and I cook cod cakes and peas regularly. Not exactly avocado and eggs, but peas are a vegetable and cod is a protein, even if they are filled with ultra-processed crap in the breadcrumbs.

And I hadn't been to the gym in three weeks. Three weeks prior to writing this profile, I'd walk on the treadmill for 30 minutes just to avoid looking like a complete dickhead, and then I'd leave. My motivation dropped to zero as soon as I saw all the 'serious' gym people. It totally killed my vibe. Which was very inconsiderate of them.

The last time I had ran was two months prior when I saw my bus put its indicators on and about to leave, and I didn't want to wait five minutes for another one. I was very proud of my two-minute sprint that morning.

I decided to stick with my profile because that was the person I wanted to pretend to be, someone who had their life together. I knew that if I met the right guy, I believed I'd start doing all those things anyway, so rather than a lie, it was a goal. I just purposefully forgot to mention that.

I was completely satisfied with my profile. I chose a picture of me partying with a cheesy grin and holding an inflatable microphone (fun times), one with my friend's dog to show that I was an animal-lover, and a selfie where I was pulling a seductive duck face, pursing my lips to make them look bigger and my cheekbones more prominent to show that I. Was. SEXY. Oh, happy days.

Click, click. And I was live. Layla and I had a giggle at some of the messages instantly pouring in, and then I went to sleep.

The next morning, I woke up to 68 more messages! Oh no, I wondered whether signing up to a dating site was a mistake? I didn't have time for this. All I wanted was maybe one to three perfect men to enter my inbox, not 68 that I didn't have time to look at that morning.

'Well, maybe I'll sift through these later when I'm back at the flat with Layla tonight and we've got some drinks flowing, so we can compare again and have a giggle,' I thought.

But at that moment… I wasn't sure that this online dating thing was for me. It was overwhelming.

After work and back at the flat, Layla and I decided to celebrate (like we did every night, to be fair—but this particular night was extra special because we were well and truly putting ourselves out there).

We were both in our pjs but decided to pop down to Sainsbury's to stock up on wine. I also grabbed a cheese twist from the bakery section (I was obsessed) and a packet of Monster Munch for later when I was starving and needed to soak up the alcohol. The cod cakes and peas didn't cut it when I was drinking, and I knew I was getting drunk.

Back up the three flights of stairs to the flat we went, giggling about some of the messages we had to sift through, full of bad communication skills and cheesy chat-up lines.

Once inside, we decided to leave the messages we had received for that evening and crank up Magic FM on the radio and have a full-on dancing session in the kitchen.

BOOM BOOM BOOM—'What the fuck is that?' I say, looking at Layla in shock. The floor was shaking. Layla, not arsed, continued dancing.

BOOM BOOM BOOM—'Layla, I think the flat below is hitting our floor with a broom!' Layla, still without a care in the world, just shrugs and says, 'It's okay,' and kept dancing.

BOOM BOOM BOOM—'Layla, someone is hitting our ceiling.'

At this point, we found it funny and stomped even louder back at them in response. We were both jumping and running heavily on the spot, and the person hitting our ceiling was getting even louder.

Suddenly, it went silent. Phew. We won—woohoo! It was time to carry on enjoying ourselves and we shrugged off the broom moment. Pulling some shapes, looking at each other and laughing, we were living in the moment without a care in the world.

But then there was a knock on the front door. We both looked at each other. We hardly ever had unexpected guests. We were whispering to one another, wondering 'Who on earth could this be? Do we answer the door?'

We answered the door.

Two slight, short men stood there with faces like thunder. The one with the reddest face shouted, 'It's 10 pm at night, it's a weeknight. We are trying to sleep, and you are having a party upstairs.'

In my drunken, happy state I was extremely offended.

He continued, 'You have knocked one of our pictures off our wall with all your stomping. Can you ask your guests to be a bit quieter?'

Layla and I exchanged mischievous looks, and I could tell she was thinking, 'Guests, what guests?'

Red Face shouts in my face, 'You all sound like a herd of elephants.'

Having once looked up rules and regulations regarding noise, I was astounded that we were being shouted at, at only 10pm at night. At this point, I lose it.

'READ YOUR RULES AND REGS, PLEASE! WE HAVE UNTIL 11 PM TONIGHT TO TURN THE MUSIC DOWN. GOODBYE,' I retort, then slammed the door shut.

I was totally appalled and drunkenly baffled that people would have the audacity to kill our vibe when it wasn't even legally the time to stop making noise and turn the music down. Party poopers.

But then, there was another knock at the door.

I answered the door again, this time with Layla hiding behind it.

I shout, 'Yes? According to Google, it says we legally have until 11 pm to turn the music off. So, we will turn the music off at 11 pm,' and in my drunken slur, I add, 'We are sticking to the rules. We are not rule-breakers ya know!'

At this point, it was just Red Face there. His mate had clearly had enough and gone back to their flat.

Red Face says, 'Are your guests going home at 11 pm then, or are you still going to be rowdy?'

'Oh man... how do I explain that two people have made enough noise for 20 of us?' I thought before answering the question.

I calmed down and finally, in a polite, more lady-like manner, said, 'Yes, they will, don't worry. My apologies, we just have a lot to celebrate. 11 pm, don't you worry, on the dot.'

And that... we never heard or saw them ever again. They may have moved out, or maybe they just put up with their picture falling off the wall most nights. But whatever the reason was, we were left to enjoy our flat (I would say in peace) the way we wanted—loud, proud, and without any thought for our neighbours. Disgraceful.

The next morning, I was at work and slumped at my desk with a grey face and probably stinking of booze from the night before. My usually blue eyes were dull and had no soul behind them. And my fake-tanned face was flushed from getting flashbacks from the night before. Now that I was sober, I had started to see how unapologetic I was for Layla and I's party for two last night. I think I was out of order. 'Oops,' I think, regretfully.

My boss, a Jewellery Buying Manager 'Lana Banana' was giving me filthy looks. Nothing unusual cos she is a walking bully, she had been taken to HR so many times in the past for treating her staff unfairly (so Tanya from Merchandising told me). I felt like sticking my middle finger up at her, but I couldn't afford to lose my job.

I left my desk and went to the photocopier room; it always had a new 'office' smell in this particular room, and it smelled good compared to the rest of the building (Unless Darren aka Mr Whiffy from accounts walked in).

I was not in the mood to work that day. But I wasn't feeling bad that I was being slower with work because I often worked late and for no extra pay. I didn't work late cos I wanted to; I only ever did because my boss scared the hell out of me.

Lana Banana was married to a high-up Head of Marketing for a prestigious high-street store. They had two children, a nanny, and lived in Surrey. On the surface, they didn't seem to have any reasons for her to be such a bitch to people. If she was happy, she wouldn't try to make other people unhappy. Happy people don't treat others badly; they don't have the energy for bad vibes. That's what I told myself anyway.

I got back to my desk and Lana Banana was seriously eyeballing me. The look that she was trying to give was to show that she wasn't happy with me, but all I could see was what she looked like constipated. She needed to work on her 'I'm not happy with you' stare because if she kept looking at people like that, she was going to need a hell of a lot of Botox. I stared back at her and smiled.

She bellowed over at me across the long 12-seater desk in a high-pitched tone, 'Lucyyyyy, did you speak to Winnie about ordering 5000 more pieces of the Isabella Sterling Silver Cubic Zirconia rings?'

Oh, shit. 'What order, Lana?'

Lana Banana huffed and loudly shouted, 'The 5000 Isabella pieces I spoke to you about... that you were meant to order on Friday.'

The whole office stared at me, approximately 30 people. I didn't remember her asking me to do this; she must have asked someone else. I always wrote everything down and never missed a thing. I wouldn't dare because she scared me so much, and I usually would never dare question her.

I started panicking. She was looking extremely angry, but she really didn't ask me to do it. It wasn't my fault, but everyone was looking at me like I was in big trouble.

Lana Banana had quite the temper, and I needed to think quick on how to react to this. Instead, I just said the only thing that I could, 'Oh, Lana, I didn't, I'm really sorry. But I don't recall you asking me to order anymore.'

The office was completely silent at this point; everyone was pretending not to watch but blatantly put work on pause to witness the office excitement in a 'non-obvious' way. But I clocked the bunch of nosey knoblets.

Lana Banana's face was about to explode. My mind was racing and all I was thinking was, 'Someone please save me; I really am worried now.'

Lana Banana barked, 'I KNOW YOU DIDN'T ORDER IT BECAUSE I CHECKED. I WANTED TO SEE WHAT YOU WOULD SAY. EITHER DO YOUR JOB OR GO HOME.'

I tried to hold back the tears, but it was too much. I ran out of the office, through the doors, turned right, and collapsed in the jewellery stock cage where we kept all our samples.

What an absolute bitch! I was slumped on the carpet, leaning against trays of crap costume jewellery (not ones I bought in), hysterically crying, and now and again a snort came out because I was uncontrollably sobbing.

I couldn't believe she embarrassed me like that. I was so upset with myself for not standing up to her further. She didn't ask me; I was 25 and I had a sharp memory. She was always forgetting so much, and I just let her walk all over me in front of everyone.

It wouldn't surprise me if she even knew that she didn't ask me and had done this on purpose to make herself feel more powerful.

I thought working for Cass-hole at the TV Shopping Channel was bad, but this was another level. Being far from my parents and loving my life in London (despite that job) I had to remain employed.

Not one person had ran after me to see if I was ok, but I knew that my colleagues just simply wouldn't dare even if they wanted to.

Five minutes had gone by, and my hysterical crying episode had calmed down. I could breathe better, but tears were silently streaming down my face.

But then, I heard footsteps. Oh no, who was it?

'Hello Lucy, are you okay?' It was Annabelle, the nosiest girl in the office. She was such a kiss-ass and would have been loving this. She was sickeningly perfect too. From California, she had the clearest, most flawless skin and shiniest dark hair I had ever seen.

'I'm not okay, Annabelle. I just feel like I can't do anything right. Lana Banana hates me and is setting me up to look like a fool and she didn't ask me to order them,' I said, pouring out my frustration.

Annabelle looked at me with a fake sympathetic expression. I was sure there was also a look on her face that almost screamed she thought I was overreacting. She tilted her head to one side and gave a little smile. 'Come on, Lucy, wipe those tears, and let's go back into the office.'

It felt like the longest walk of my life, walking up the steps next to Annabelle. As we walked through the aisle of the office, Annabelle went back to her perfectly clean and tidy desk. The office was silent, with everyone again pretending to be really busy and not looking at me, but they were. Tears continued to roll down my face.

Lana Banana was at her desk with the sternest look on her face, not looking up. I took a deep breath and walked over to her. 'Lana, please can I have a word with you?'

With no expression on her face, she replied coldly, 'Yes, you may.'

Tears became more frequent again. 'I am so sorry, Lana, for running off like that, but I am adamant you didn't ask me to order them. I would admit it if you had, but you didn't. You can see I am clearly upset.'

Lana huffed. 'I know you are upset, Lucy, but so am I. We needed that stock for the Happy Days deal weekend, and now it won't arrive on time, so we will have to think of another plan. I will leave that with you. Don't let me down AGAIN.'

For heaven's sake, she would never admit she was wrong and forgot to ask me to order them. I bloody hated her.

As I trudged through the remainder of the workday, my mind drifted constantly to 5 pm when I could get the hell out of there.

The weight of the day's events hung heavy on my shoulders, and I couldn't shake off the events of the day. Each passing minute felt like an eternity, every task an obstacle to overcome before I could finally escape and find refuge in mine and Layla's flat with a bottle of wine.

The weekend arrived and a sense of determination settled within me. I had reached my breaking point with my boss, and her bullying and nastiness had become unbearable. The once-exciting world of fashion and buying now felt suffocating because of 'Lana Banana,' and I knew I could no longer cope with the misery she inflicted on my daily life; it was making me feel weak and voiceless. I wanted out.

I set out for Dalston and the weight of my decision was heavy on my shoulders. Tears streamed down my face as I walked along the familiar streets and called my dad, crying my eyes out. I got the occasional second glance from people, but it was obvious they had seen others like this before. I felt alone in my distress of not knowing what to do, and my dad had always been my biggest motivator and solution finder.

As I listened to my dad's comforting words, his unwavering support offered hope. He had offered to help me look for jobs to apply for in London and to stick it out with my head held high until I found another job. With his encouragement, I felt stronger and knew that I would find a way out of that suffocating situation and feel happier. I just wanted to work for a nice person who didn't have power issues—was it that hard to find?

Chapter Fourteen

King-Ding-a-Long

LAYLA

Hot days on the tube were the worst. Packed in like baked beans on a busy commuter tube, the stench of body odour filled the air, making you feel like you might disintegrate into a puddle of liquid. One particular sweltering day, I foolishly decided to wear my Ugg boots. It was the middle of summer, and I had chosen fur-lined sheepskin boots! I can't remember the logic behind that decision, but there must have been some reason.

Anyway, it was a workday, a Friday morning to be precise and the humidity was unbearable. Even walking to the station, I could feel sweat starting to seep out of my pores.

I stepped onto the tube, and it was packed as usual. The doors closed, and the heat enveloped me, making it hard to breathe. There was nowhere to sit, so I ended up standing directly under the armpit of a very tall man, my nose practically squashed against it. It didn't smell good, and I was stifling the urge to gag.

My body was sweating, and I started to notice a tingling sensation in my feet—no, not tingling, wet. Yep, a puddle of watery sweat was forming in my boots.

Shit. I had to get off the tube and walk to work in those!

The tube pulled into my stop, and there was no choice but to take the plunge. I set off through Oxford Circus, squelching with every step. After what felt like the longest journey ever (it was a ten-minute walk), I finally got to work and went straight to the toilets. I sat in a cubicle, took off the boots, and to my horror, not only were they swimming in sweat, but they also stank! I was mortified.

I was pretty sure everyone at work could smell my feet. If they didn't, they could certainly hear me squelching around the office. Every step sounded like I had a mini whoopee cushion stuffed down each boot.

My Uggs never recovered from that fateful day. Someone told me to sprinkle them with baking soda to alleviate the smell. All it did was turn the lovely white sheepskin a dirty shade of yellow, and yes, they still smelled.

Thank fuck it was nearly the weekend and I had two full days to live down the embarrassment, drink some wine and forget about it.

Lucy and I had a night out planned in Islington that evening with her friend Kerrie who was coming to visit, I knew that this night-out would take my mind off of that cringe-worthy moment. I was counting on it.

Approximately 12 hours later…

It was the morning after the night out, my head was pounding and my mouth dry. I had a sinking feeling that I was not alone.

Turning over, my worst fears were confirmed: sprawled out beside me in all his glory was a grubby-looking bloke, grinning smugly. 'Good morning,' he said, his tone far too cheerful for my liking. My mind raced, trying to piece together the events of last night and coming up frustratingly blank. MY GOD! WHAT HAD I DONE THIS TIME?

From the other bedroom, I heard Lucy and Kerrie happily chatting away. They were my lifelines in this moment because they were the only ones who would be able to fill in the gaps of my memory from the night before.

But at that moment, I couldn't bear to face them. With a groan, I buried my head in the pillow, desperately wishing I could turn back the clock and undo whatever foolishness had led me to this moment.

But I knew that I had to face reality soon because I was sleeping next to a man proudly lying there like he was King-Ding-a-Long, when he was anything but that.

So, rewinding 12 hours to the night before, I vaguely recalled that we had headed over to Islington. I thought we ended up at a bar... The Piano Bar, that's it!

I wondered whether this was where this grungy-looking stray came into the picture, surely! Truth be told, my memory of the evening abruptly ended after my fourth margarita. I had always been one to go big or go home; I had never been able to 'pace myself' when it came to drinking.

I thought I met him while ordering drinks, and I thought we got chatting from there. As for the conversation, who knew? With his dishevelled appearance—trilby hat and skinny faded jeans—he was definitely not my usual type. This guy must have really charmed me with his sparkling personality! I was sure the shots and margaritas helped!

I heard Lucy and Kerrie moving from the bedroom into the living room. It was time to face the music and find out if all this detective work, I was doing in my head was true.

It turned out that much of my interpretation of last night's events were true. The only thing I could not work out was how we had left and how he had ended up back in the flat with me.

Lucy and Kerrie whispered to me what went down while King-Ding-a-Long was having a morning wee.

According to Lucy and Kerrie, I had bolted with him from the bar. Sounds about right. They chased me down the street, obviously worried, and tried to talk me out of it, as Lucy had known I would regret it in the morning. But I had none of it and was determined to go ahead with my plan, and I would not let them stop me!

As they were chasing me down the street, they saw me stop and snog King-Ding-a-Long up against a lamppost. In my tipsy state, I hit my head back against the lamppost. No wonder my head felt so sore.

The problem I had was that this bloke did not want to leave! So, as an escape tactic, Lucy and Kerrie had suggested going out for breakfast at The Rochester Castle, a Wetherspoons pub in Stoke Newington. This was exactly what I was craving: a big, greasy fry-up with a strong mug of tea, complete with a spoon standing upright (as anyone who has ever had tea in a London café knows).

Unfortunately, King-Ding-a-Long had taken this as an invite. God knows how, as Lucy had made it very clear—especially after she had found him later lying on the sofa with his greasy hair on top of one of her freshly ironed work outfits. She had ripped it from his smelly, unwashed head—this moment should have been obvious to him that he was definitely not invited!

I was so hungover, and probably still a bit tipsy, that my brain was not equipped to deal with that morning-after-the-night-before awkward situation. I wanted to be the suave, sophisticated London girl and tell him with a firm but casual air that last night had been fun, but it was really time for him to leave.

I made an excuse and skulked off to Lucy's bedroom for help once again. Lucy was not fazed by this problem; she told me that she would just tell him straight on my behalf that he wasn't invited!

A few minutes later, we all headed out onto the high street. Just as he was about to follow us across the road to the pub, Lucy turned to him and said, 'Um, sorry, where are you going?' He looked at her with his grubby grin, obviously thinking she was joking. 'I'm coming to breakfast with you.'

'No, sorry, you're not invited! Girls only!' Lucy declared, cutting off any further discussion.

A little while later, we were sat in the pub, ordering a nice big greasy fry-up, with Lucy and Kerrie absolutely pissing themselves at me across the table, recounting the traumatizing sounds they had overheard from the night before. I was cringing and shrinking smaller and smaller into my seat. Those flat walls were thin; thank the lord I was too drunk to fully remember it all myself.

Irresponsible way to look at it, I know, but I was in my 20s and had watched far too much *Sex and the City*. It had become the benchmark for life. Samantha would not give a damn, so why should I? The only difference was, Samantha would go on a shopping spree down Fifth Avenue to avenge her misdemeanours, whereas I was sat in Wetherspoons in Stoke Newington, licking my wounds.

Later that afternoon, Lucy and I were back at the flat, Kerrie having left to catch the train home. When we had no plans on a Sunday afternoon, a normal routine would include a flat spring-clean and a blast of Magic FM.

After having a greasy, grubby man stay over, it was needed. The air smelled musty and pungent; he had certainly left his scent, one I did not want to continue to inhale, nor did Lucy.

We cracked the windows and emptied the cupboard under the sink of cleaning products. Out came the air freshener and disinfectant, with me scrubbing vigorously at the cream leather sofa and her doing her usual dance with the mop.

She used to kill me with that mop; she would appear from nowhere with it, singing into it like a microphone, then do some sort of backwards dance-shuffle disappearing down the other end of the hallway.

After the fumigation had taken place, it was time to relax. This would often involve wine and crisps; living above a Sainsbury's Local had its advantages all the time. So, we trotted downstairs to stock up.

We had become quite well-known with the Sainsbury's staff, and whenever we went in, they would pop over and have a chat, eager to hear the gossip about what we had been up to on our nights out because there was always, usually some story we had to tell and we loved telling them a story, keeping them entertained on their shift. Well, this was one occasion I was not going to spill!

Back at work that week, and not one to dwell on a disastrous weekend, I had signed up to a dating site linked through one of the London free papers. Yes, back in the early noughties, that really was a thing! Anyway, I hadn't had much interaction with anyone via this site—well, up until now!

I had received a new 'like' and message with a profile picture, and this guy was FIT! Dark features and a gorgeous smile, he was a world away from the haggard-looking stray I had picked up the weekend before.

His name was George, and he lived in Clapton in Hackney, a mere 10 minutes away! Being young, naive, and completely overexcited, I did not need to know any more. We exchanged pleasantries and very quickly arranged a date for Friday night that week. He had offered to come over to Stokey and meet in the Three Crowns pub, so all that was left for me to do was prepare for the date.

Working for a fashion brand meant I had options with my outfit, although it still did not stop me from trying on every single item in my wardrobe (and half of Lucy's too). I ended up reverting back to outfit number one (we have all been there)—a pair of jeans and a blue blouse. Smart but casual, it looked like I had made an effort but not tried too hard.

After getting ready, Lucy and I cracked open the wine and I sank a couple of glasses to curb the pre-date nerves with Gorgeous George.

Afterwards, feeling slightly tipsy, I tottered off down the high street to meet my match. I remember I had put on a huge pair of black cork wedges that I could barely walk in (I rarely did heels), and before I had even reached the end of the road, my feet were beginning to ache.

I knew Gorgeous George had already arrived as he had texted me and asked what I wanted to drink. So, when I entered the pub, nerves a-go-go, I saw him sitting there, looking every bit the adonis: tall, dark, and very, very handsome. I melted there and then.

How was I going to keep my composure and stop myself from dribbling and drooling into my drink? Turns out, George was not only easy on the eye, but he was also chatty, interesting, and funny.

I wanted to slap myself around the face; this was a totally new experience to what I was used to.

At the end of the night, Gorgeous George walked me back to the flat, minus a pair of clumpy wedges that were now slung over my shoulder, classy as always. I probably invited him up, as I wasn't great with boundaries, lol.

However, instead, we left it there and said our goodbyes on the doorstep. We had a drunken kiss, with me standing barefoot on tiptoes and no doubt swaying a lot.

Afterwards, I was on cloud nine and sauntered up those three flights of stairs like I was walking on water, bursting through the flat door and into the living room, declaring to Lucy, 'I have found the one, I am in love!!!'

I proceeded to see Gorgeous George intensely for the next few months. It was all very full-on, but I was in rose-tinted spectacle mode and had no intentions of taking things slow. If Gorgeous George asked to see me, I would immediately cancel all plans and go running.

We met up in the evenings after work and got together on weekends. I began staying around his flat, even on weeknights. Hell, he even got me my very own pink toothbrush!

I really was starting to feel like one of those smug London couples I had lusted after, wandering around together looking fantastic and insanely happy and in love.

Then slowly, Gorgeous George began going a bit cold on me. Well, a lot cold. We would arrange to have a night together, and at the last minute, he would cancel, using work or something else as an excuse. I could not work out why.

Nothing bad had happened, no big argument. The last time I had seen him, it was a lovely night in at his, watching a movie with a takeaway. We got up and ready for work the next morning; he walked me to the bus stop, kissed me, and waved me off. All was good. It was puzzling.

Eventually, Gorgeous George stopped contacting me completely. I sent the odd message to him; however, he never replied. I was heartbroken.

I spent the next couple of months in turmoil, walking around with my jaw on the floor, desperately hoping Gorgeous George would get back in contact and tell me he was sorry and that he had made a terrible mistake, that he was madly in love with me and wanted to have my babies.

Did that happen in reality? Of course it did not. Lucy was my rock, my shoulder to cry on, and spent many a night in the flat with me, mopping up my snotty tears and plying me with wine. She let me go over it all again and again, trying to make sense of what the fuck had happened.

Sensing my sadness my mum and dad came down to stay the following weekend. They loved me taking them on adventures around London and were very impressed with my 'London Underground knowledge' (te he), so they trusted me to get us from A to B.

On this occasion, I decided we'd have a little mooch around the West End. I wanted to show them where I worked and take them for a walk around Soho. We got on the tube at Finsbury Park and headed to Oxford Circus.

Everything went smoothly as we wandered around Soho, and then I suggested we jump back on the tube and go the short distance to St. James's Park. My dad had taken to hopping on and off the tubes easily, keeping up with the fast-paced Londoners rushing by. Mum, however, struggled with the speed. Dad and I made it through the doors, which shut tight, and the tube moved off.

I turned to Dad and asked, 'Where's Mum?' We turned around and saw her panic-stricken face still on the platform! All we could do was wave at her as we sailed off into the tunnel.

In my head, I was thinking, do we go back? Do we get off at the next station and wait? We may NEVER find her again! Well, at least not for a few hours.

In the end, we decided to get off at the next stop and hope that she had got on the tube behind us. Thankfully, she had, and we were reunited once more! After my mum was returned to us, we were all in fits of giggles and it was the first time I had belly-laughed so hard since Gorgeous George doing a disappearing act on me.

Over time though, I picked myself back up, reminding myself I was a young twenty-something girl and living my London dream. I had a great job working in Soho, lots of friends, and so it wasn't worth getting that upset about.

I had also recently joined the YMCA gym on Tottenham Court Road and for the first time in my life, was enjoying 'working out'. So, I threw myself into that, my job, and of course, nights out.

Although I moved on, I never really did get over Gorgeous George properly. Of course, I went on many more dates, but nobody really measured up, and of course, I was always comparing.

An embarrassing side note, not so long after and after a fair few too many drinks at home alone, I started thinking about Gorgeous George and desperately wanted to see him. Cue a drunken bike ride from Stokey to Clapton! I pedalled drunkenly down to his estate in the dead of night, over to the block of flats where he lived. I stopped on the pavement and stared up at his flat window, hoping to catch a glimpse of him. God only knows what I must have looked like to passersby!

I literally had no game plan either; I hadn't thought that far ahead. If he had seen me, he would no doubt have been terrified to witness this crazy ex of a stalker lurking in the shadows on a mountain bike, glaring up through his window. Not exactly the best way to win him over.

Chapter Fifteen

Treading on Thin Ice

LUCY

Amongst the heaps of men on the dating site, I had finally found a connection with one called Ben. He lived in Manchester but was moving to London. It felt like fate that he was moving to my stomping ground. He had family in London and was job hunting, planning to move in with his cousin in Brixton. I mean, he could have moved in with Layla and me, but I tried not to get ahead of myself.

He sounded normal and funny. We were constantly texting throughout the day, and then he asked if I wanted to meet up that weekend. Fuck.

Kerrie was coming down that weekend, and we'd had plans in place for months. We were all set to go to The Ice Bar in Leicester Square. I was sure she wouldn't mind being a third wheel for an hour afterwards. Kerrie was quite the socialite and got along with most people, so I knew that she wouldn't dampen the vibe.

Ben was visiting his family, so I didn't think he would want to stay out too long, which meant Kerrie and I could still have our girls' night. There I was, trying to juggle a man and my friends. I could already feel it becoming a constant reality. It was so bloody stressful, but I loved it.

Everything was set, and Kerrie was thrilled for me that I had a date. She was in a relationship and eager for me to find someone so that we could go on double dates.

It was Friday night, the day of THE date. Kerrie was on her way to the flat, and I was so excited to see her. We loved the milkshakes from a café up the road, and Kerrie had offered to pick some up for her, Layla and me.

Thinking back, we had been pretty lazy. Kerrie had travelled an hour and a half, whilst Layla and I spent the morning in the flat recovering from the previous night's drinking, and me drunkenly texting Ben (ignoring the other guys that were messaging since Ben seemed to be ticking all the boxes).

When Kerrie arrived, I buzzed her into the flat. Five minutes later, she knocked on the door, covered in milkshake. She had tripped on one of the flights of stairs, and the milkshakes had gone all over the walls and Kerrie. Not surprising, considering she was trying to carry three milkshakes, an overnight bag, and a plastic carrier bag with booze in it.

Kerrie cleaned herself up, and after I asked Layla and Kerrie about ten times if I looked okay and if I looked like my pictures, we finally headed out. I even asked them to take a photo of me with my pink Fujifilm camera. Mirrors can be deceiving, and my perception of myself varied with my mood—I could either feel that I looked okay or that I resembled Miss Trunchbull.

Kerrie and I had a great time at the Ice Bar, and I was buzzing to meet Ben. As we walked out of the Ice Bar, we headed to the bar where I was meeting him.

We sat outside and headed for some wooden bench tables, each with a drink in hand, as it wasn't yet time to meet him. We decided to sit at one of the tables and get comfy.

Kerrie planned to leave just before 7 PM, the time I was meeting Ben, and head to the shops, giving Ben and I time to meet and bond. I told Kerrie to walk past five minutes later, and if I stuck my arm up in the air, it would be a sign for her to come back and rescue me.

The time came. Kerrie wished me luck and walked off into the distance. I was feeling apprehensive as a short man, much heavier than in his profile pictures, started walking towards me.

WTH, this man wasn't the same as in his photos. No way. His face was totally different. He wasn't 'my type' at all. I didn't find him remotely attractive, not like the man in the pictures. But, trying to be polite, I decided to go with it.

He greeted me in a very relaxed manner, almost rude, and looked straight through me. I wasn't sure who was behind his eyes. He sat down at the table without getting a drink or asking if I wanted one. It felt very bizarre, but maybe he was just nervous. I wasn't sure.

The conversation was slow. Normally a chatterbox, I could usually make conversation with anyone, but this guy was really testing my communication skills and there were many long silences.

I stuck my hand up in the air, explaining to Ben that I sometimes got a restless arm, and this was how I got relief. Then I started waving it around in the air, SOS style. People at other tables looked at me, but I didn't care; I needed help.

This was quite possibly the worst date I had ever been on. I couldn't see Kerrie anywhere. Oh goodness, help me, please. In desperation, I raised my other arm and started waving both arms like I was at a concert. Kerrie walked out of a shop, noticed me, and quickened her pace back to the table. Thank goodness for that. I didn't have to look like a prat any longer.

As Kerrie returned and introduced herself to this imbecile, she gave me a knowing look that clearly said she could tell I didn't like this man. To start a conversation, Kerrie told Ben about our time at the Ice Bar.

Ben proceeded to say, 'The thing is, the bar isn't actually made of ice.'

Frustrated, I insisted, 'Yes, it is.'

He replied, 'No, it isn't, because ya see this table we're sitting at now? If it was made of ice, it would melt. And if the bar was made of ice, it would all melt.'

Kerrie looked at me, smirked, and her shoulders started shaking—I could tell she was on the verge of bursting into laughter.

Feeling frustrated and putting on a very serious (as if I was some sort of scientist) voice, I explained to him that the bar is indeed completely made of ice, maintained at a specific temperature to prevent melting—precisely -5 degrees Celsius. That's why they provided us with gloves and an Ice Bar coat.

The table we were sitting at outside wasn't made of ice, and if it were, yes, it would melt because the outdoor temperature wasn't cold enough to keep it from melting.

I was dealing with a nutcase here. Not only was he not the man from his pictures, but he was also a complete melt (pun intended).

His reply to my clever explanation was, 'No, no, no, the thing is… it would all melt, because ice melts.'

Oh my… was this man living in cuckoo land? I couldn't believe it. Seeing how frustrated I was, Kerrie decided to pretend to agree with him, smirking as she said, 'Yes, he's right, Lucy. Ice melts.'

I looked at her with a smile of frustration, knowing she was just playing along.

'I give up. Anyway, Ben, it was nice to meet you, but could you kindly fuck off back to weirdo land and leave me to have a night with my friend?'

Alright, I didn't actually say that, but I was tempted to. I simply sighed and said, 'Okay, I give up trying to convince you both. Ben, it was nice to meet you, but unfortunately, we have to go now,' glancing at Kerrie with a pleading look. True to form, she went along with it, and we got up from the table and left.

We giggled about the absurdity of it all on the tube ride back to the flat.

I never heard from Ben again. Thank fuck.

Kerrie was staying for two nights, so we decided to go back home, get our heads down and plan a night out for the Saturday night.

The next morning, we decided to go to Muswell Hill, we'd been there the month before, when we met some randoms at the Red Lion in Stoke Newington and they decided to give us a lift to a pub with a dance floor that they recommended.

Squeezed into an Audi TT, me Kerrie, Layla and Grace couldn't all fit in the back with the two guys taking us. So, the smallest of the 5-footers Kerrie and Layla sat in the footwells with mine and Grace putting our feet over them for comfort.

As we travelled the 18 minutes at 11pm at night, we were relieved to finally get there. Although we all found the situation we were in funny as fuck. As soon as they dropped us off, we were no longer interested in them so after they bought us a first drink, we hit the dance floor and didn't see them for the rest of the evening.

Remembering how we had a good time, Kerrie and I got dressed up and got a taxi to the same place. I remember having a great night of dancing, chatting to randoms and feeling in my element.

By the end of the night, we were starving. So, we headed over the road to the local kebab shop. As we entered, I immediately clocked a very goodlooking, slightly short but dreamy guy. We looked at one another and I could feel the mutual interest.

Trying to be cool I ordered my doner kebab and chips and only looked at him now and again. But when he walked by, he pinched my bum, and I knew it was game on.

'Oi cheeky' I said in a flirtatious way and with that we started talking and he invited Kerrie and I to an after-party.

Of course, we agreed, and they said they would give us a lift as it was in Brixton in South London and currently being North of the River, it would take us forever to get there by tube.

There was approximately 6 of them, and as we walked back to their cars. One of the men that was with my crush asks my name and I tell him. I ask what his name is too, in a polite way (as I like his friend and want to get on with his friends) and he replied 'Toilet'.

Puzzled, I said 'Really?' and with that response he gets aggressive and started calling me a 'stupid bitch.' He started fronting me as if I was a man and wanted to start a fight. Alarm bells should have rung at this point. But they didn't.

I wanted to slap him with my handbag!! My crush and two of his other friend's stepped-in front of him and told him to back off. He did. He was definitely the runt of the friendship group.

Kerrie and I walked off to the car with my crush and his two friends.

'Toilet' and the other two went their separate ways and I just hoped that they wouldn't be at the after party. When we arrived at their car it was an expensive Range Rover with blacked out windows. 'Oh goodness, they're footballers,' i thought. Not ideal, but at least they aren't dodgy.

Kerrie and I, who were completely naïve, got into the car and were driven to a party in Brixton. We pulled up to some high-rise flats, and Crush mentioned he needed to take his dogs out. He told us to wait in the car and that he would let us know when we could come in.

He left the car, and a while later returned outside with two dogs. Kerrie mouthed to me, 'These dogs are illegal, Lucy.' Intoxicated and knowing nothing about dogs, I didn't realise the seriousness of illegal dogs.

Crush took the dogs back inside and then returned to let us in. His friend didn't come with us. What kind of party was this? Crush led us to his bedroom, where Kerrie and I sat on his bed. There was a dog in a cage staring at us, and we could hear dogs barking from the kitchen.

He started talking about all the dodgy things that he was involved in (what was this man on? We could have been undercover police officers). Instead, we were just two silly girls who believed we were going to an after-party.

A party for three plus three illegal dogs. What was this?

Crush left the room, and Kerrie and I exchanged nervous glances, agreeing that we needed to get out of there. But before we could escape, there was a knock at the door. Oh, my goodness, what was going to happen to us?

It turned out to be his friend dropping off what I assumed were drugs. Luckily, he didn't come in.

We made our excuses, I swapped numbers with Crush (why?), and we left. As we walked to the tube station, I realized I had forgotten my faux leather jacket.

Instead of just buying a new jacket, the next day, I texted Crush to ask if I could collect it. He agreed, so Kerrie and I set off in the KA back to Brixton. Brixton is usually busy, but this day the roads were chock-a-block. We were stuck behind a long line of cars in one lane, while the lane next to us was moving fast. I signalled to change lanes, but no one would let me in.

We sat there for about 20 minutes, waiting for our lane to move or for someone to let us in, only for Kerrie to realize and say, 'Lucy, we're stuck behind parked cars. No one is in the cars in front of us.'

Once I collected my jacket, I vowed never to return to Brixton again.

Despite Kerrie and I not being very 'street' coming from a small market town, we weren't strangers to dodgy situations. When we were 21, we went on a girls' holiday to Rhodes with our friends Katy and Grace.

We had booked two apartments in the complex, with Kerrie and me sharing one. While Katy and Grace's apartment was lovely and spacious, ours looked like it was straight out of a horror movie—cracked windows and backing onto an open field.

We both had a bad feeling about it. Given our love for horror films, we were convinced we'd end up as the main characters in a murder scene if we stayed in that room.

We didn't waste any time sharing our concerns about the room with the resort owner. He responded, in a thick Greek accent, 'I cannot move you because of a feeling.'

Undeterred, Kerrie passionately declared that we wouldn't stay in that room and suggested we could ask her dad to borrow his credit card to book elsewhere if necessary.

The owner, clearly fed up with our dramatics, finally moved us to a much nicer room. But he also told us that we weren't to be alarmed by a man walking around the resort with a gun and it's for our protection. WTF!

We were also not allowed to bring anyone from outside of the resort into the establishment, and we were not allowed to mix in our rooms with any boys from the resort. Bloody hell, fun police alert!

We got chatting with some of the other residents, and they casually mentioned that the owner was part of the mafia. That explained why 'Darren' the gunman strolled around the resort with a gun slung over his shoulder. Nice guy, really, but with his stocky build and lack of facial expressions, you could tell he didn't tolerate any shit.

One night, we went to an R&B bar, and I met the most handsome man named Luke. He was 6ft and had a face that could have graced a magazine cover. A footballer and 30 years old, he was a bit older than me. He seemed to like me, and we exchanged numbers, agreeing to meet up the next night with our friends.

We did, and it was brilliant. I was high on life meeting this guy. Later on in the evening, Kerrie, Grace, and Katy headed back to the apartments, and I was in my element staying out with the boys.

At the end of the night, he offered to drive me back on a quad bike he had hired. We hopped on and I felt incredibly cool. 'Check me out on this fitties quad bike,' I thought.

As we neared the resort, I warned him to drop me off outside because Darren had a gun and didn't allow outsiders in. He didn't take me seriously and drove right in.

Out of nowhere, Darren appeared, pointing his gun at his head. I quickly told him to leave and apologized to Darren like a guilty child, 'I'm so sorry, Darren. I told him not to come in, but he didn't believe me about the gun.'

Darren looked at me with a straight face, but I could see a glint of humour in his eyes, almost like a Buckingham Palace guard trying not to laugh.

A day or so later, we made friends with some of the lads around the pool. By then, Luke had gone home, and we'd agreed to meet up when I was back in the UK. Some of the lads around the pool were single and some were in relationships.

I fancied one of them named Mark. He was tall, with brown hair, blue eyes, and a tan that would make a coconut jealous. I never made it known, but I was giggly around him and I would catch myself staring at him.

Anyway, some of the lads came into Kerrie's and my apartment to play cards (100% innocent) on our balcony. Literally within minutes, Darren appeared with his gun. 'Boys, get out now.' FFS Darren!

The mafia man lived at the resort with his wife and children. They were very welcoming. One night, the mafia man told us we couldn't use the bar because he was having the chief of police and some officers round for a hog roast. Because nothing says 'relaxing holiday' like sharing a resort with the local mafia and their best pals, the police. It was surreal.

The even weirder thing was that Katy had a friend who had been a holiday rep at this exact resort. While we were out there, she texted him, and he told her that the room Kerrie and I were initially meant to stay in had a lad who sadly died in that apartment whilst on holiday.

No wonder we had a strong, uneasy feeling in there. I'd always thought I was a little psychic at times, but at this point I was convinced Kerrie also had this trait.

So, if we did possess this psychic trait, how on earth did we both end up in this dodgy apartment in Brixton, just the three of us, when we were supposed to be at a fucking party?! Clearly, our psychic radar must've taken the night off - if it was even there at all.

In the midst of Kerrie and I's lucky escape from the 'after-party,' my dad had kindly been searching for jobs for me and sending me links to apply. He found a job as a proof-reader for a publishing company in Balham, South London and it looked something that I could transfer my skills to.

After a week, I had the interview and thankfully bagged the job. It was going to be a bit more of a trek to get to work every morning, but I was ecstatic, and this didn't phase me.

The following Monday I handed in my notice to my boss, a sense of satisfaction washed over me. Watching her reaction as she read the resignation letter was truly delightful – she cried! After enduring 12 months of her making my life miserable, and believing she had some strange animosity towards me, it was weird and shocking to see her emotional response.

As I explained my decision to leave and pursue a new path, I sensed a shift in the dynamic between us. It was as if a weight had been lifted, and I realized that beneath her tough exterior, she might have actually liked me all along.

I shared my plans to revisit my roots in journalism and media by taking on the proof-reading role. It felt liberating to declare my intentions openly, to reclaim my sense of purpose and direction after that time working for her, feeling trapped in a toxic environment.

She told me that she was jealous that I was young enough to start again, and how unhappy she was in her job. As she continued to open up about her own struggles and frustrations, a wave of empathy washed over me. Despite her bullying behaviour, I could not help but see her in a new light – as a person that was burdened by her own insecurities and unhappiness.

Listening to her confide in me about her feelings of being trapped in a job she despised, shackled by financial responsibilities like an expensive mortgage and the needs of her nanny, I felt a little bit of sympathy. It became clear that her harsh treatment of me was more about projecting her own frustrations onto me than anything else. It did calm my anger and resentment towards her.

But, despite this newfound understanding, I still couldn't help but indulge in the odd daydream of encountering her years later on the tube – confident in my own right – and finally having the opportunity to confront her about her behaviour and to be dramatic slap her round the face and walk off like I was in some sort of film.

While revenge fantasies offered a small sense of satisfaction, deep down, I knew that true closure would come from letting go of any anger towards her and moving forward with my own life. For my own sake. And so, I let it go.

Whilst our encounter may have initially had tension and conflict, I realised that not everything should be taken personally and that I must rise above toxic traits in people and protect myself emotionally.

I started my new job as a proof-reader, and I was so happy. Everyone was lovely. From the director of the company to the bosses, managers, and art workers, there wasn't a single overinflated ego in sight. Instead, I found myself surrounded by colleagues who were supportive, down-to-earth, and genuinely invested in the work we were doing.

My team-leader Mr Moon was one of the funniest, kindest people I had ever met. On my first day he was training me, and I was still getting used to the fact that I was no longer surrounded by judgemental Lana Banana.

Mr Moon sat next to me at the computer, he was showing me a document where I had to fill out the proof-reading jobs that we had done that morning, so we were keeping a record. Mr Moon was telling me what to type out on this document and then, unexpectedly, Mr. Moon told me to type out a particular spelling and then he uttered the word 'apostrophe.'

In that moment, my mind went blank. Despite the fact I was meant to be a proofreader, I couldn't, for the life of me, recall what an 'apostrophe' was. Panic seized me as I grappled with the embarrassment of not knowing a fundamental aspect of my job. It felt as though all eyes were on me and I was worrying that everyone in the office would be questioning my competence.

'Apostrophe,' Mr. Moon repeated, his voice raised slightly in volume as he assumed I hadn't heard him the first time. Panic threatened to overwhelm me as I struggled to be able to think what an apostrophe was and where to find it on the keyboard. I felt a flush of embarrassment creeping up my neck. How the fuck was I meant to be a proofreader when I couldn't even tell you what an apostrophe was?

But before I could spiral further into self-doubt, Mr. Moon repeated himself again louder than the last time 'An apostrophe?' asking in a way that he was unsure why I am not pressing the button. He eventually leaned over and pressed the apostrophe key for me. Aha of course! I explained that I had a memory blank, and we both laughed.

This forged the beginning of mine and Mr Moon's friendship. Being around Mr Moon and his team, was such a contrast from Lana Banana. I finally felt at home in the workplace working with people who were my kind of people – kind, humble and ambitious people. Life was feeling good.

When we first moved into the flat, Layla discovered a Christmas tree wedged between the fridge and the wall, missing a stand—thanks to the previous tenants. Instead of throwing it out like normal people, we decided to keep it.

Come Christmas, rather than spending money on a new tree, Layla had a stroke of genius. Using one of Layla's empty baked beans cans, we rinsed it out, and wrapped it in tinfoil like we were making a DIY masterpiece. The tin-foil-covered baked bean can held-up the Christmas tree like a champ, and we were ridiculously proud of our handiwork. Our flat looked festive, in that 'we're too broke to care' sort of way.

For New Years Eve Layla and I bought tickets to one of Trevor Nelson's R&B parties. Grace and Kerrie also got tickets, and we were all excited to celebrate together. It was snowing that particular night, we had pre-drinks in the flat and then we all ventured out into the cold ready to have a great night.

As soon as we got inside of the venue, I realized the alcohol had completely taken over Layla's brain. The atmosphere was electric, and Layla made a beeline straight for Trevor Nelson, who was on the decks, and parked herself right next to the DJ booth. She looked like she was in a trance, unable to peel her eyes off him, as if he was about to make an announcement that he was single and looking for a girlfriend.

Grace, Kerrie, and I wanted to grab a drink, so I asked Layla if she wanted to join us. 'I'm staying here,' she slurred, clearly in her happy place.

I told her we'd grab her a drink and be right back. But, of course, the queue at the bar was massive, and we ended up waiting much longer than planned. We had a dance whilst waiting and got chatting to lots of people in the queue and I assumed Layla was still being mesmerised by Trevor Nelson.

By the time we finally got our drinks and returned to the DJ booth, Layla was nowhere to be seen.

I pulled out my phone and saw two voicemails from Layla. The first one simply said, 'You're shit.'

In the second voicemail, she'd apparently decided that needed further clarification: 'You're a shit friend. I tried looking for you and couldn't find you.'

I called her, and she informed me that she'd left in a taxi. Panic set in, it was snowing, New Years Eve and I had the key to the flat. We sometimes decided that only one of us needed to take a key out when we would be together.

I asked her where she was, and she casually mentioned that someone had let her into our block of flats, and she was now sitting on the steps.

We rushed back in a taxi to find Layla, and there she was, sitting on the steps, blissfully enjoying some cheesy chips like it was the best New Year's feast ever. She had completely forgotten we were getting her a drink and, apparently, where we were too.

Chapter Sixteen

Shrek and Spok

LAYLA

It was the morning after my 28th birthday Mexican party, I woke up still feeling the lingering effects of tequila and burritos in my system. As I staggered into the living room, I found Lucy already sitting with a cup of tea, a mischievous sparkle in her eyes and a smirk on her face. I could tell she was bursting to share something with me. Her expression giving it away before she even uttered a word.

I made myself a cup of tea and eagerly settled down on the sofa. Lucy couldn't contain her excitement, her eyes twinkling with anticipation. 'Sooooo, how are you feeling about meeting the love of your life last night?' she teased, before bursting into a fit of giggles.

My heart skipped a beat as I frantically tried to recall the events of the previous night. 'Wait, what?' I responded, a mixture of confusion and anxiety creeping in.

My face must have been a picture, frantically scanning my mind, trying desperately to remember. 'No joke, you were head over heels for this bloke! Practically foaming at the mouth!' Lucy exclaimed, barely able to contain her laughter. I started to feel a little bit sick, imagining myself draped all over the poor guy in all my drunken splendour.

As Lucy's words sank in, my mind raced, desperately trying to piece together the events of the previous night. 'Head over heels for this bloke? Practically foaming at the mouth?' I repeated in disbelief and a wave of nausea washed over me as I pictured myself in that state.

Apparently, before meeting the love of my life, I somehow managed to kiss an old man on the lips in front of his wife in a packed restaurant. Here's how it went down: Lucy had secretly arranged for the staff to bring out a cake, and suddenly, the entire restaurant was singing 'Happy Birthday' to me.

In the midst of all the excitement, a gentleman in his 70s, who was dining with his wife, got up to give me a hug and politely wish me Happy Birthday. Now, in my high-on-life tipsy state from having such a fantastic night, something in my brain didn't quite function properly.

When he came in for the hug, I grabbed his face and planted a full-on kiss right on his lips.

Of course, Lucy, being Lucy, captured the entire thing on camera. When I saw the picture, there was no denying it—it was definitely me.

After quickly leaving the Mexican restaurant—or perhaps getting kicked out—we made our way up the road to the Three Crowns Pub. It was a popular spot among the local Stokey hipsters, and I vaguely recalled heading there to keep the party going. But the memory of meeting the supposed love of my life was a complete blank, much to my frustration.

'For fuck's sake,' I muttered under my breath, feeling a mix of embarrassment and annoyance at my lack of recollection. But beneath that, a flicker of excitement stirred. Could it be that I had finally met someone I could truly like?

As Lucy continued to divulge details from the previous night, it became painfully clear that I had indeed hit it off with this guy, to the point of openly snogging each other's faces off in the middle of the pub. The realization sent a shiver down my spine, accompanied by an overwhelming sense of embarrassment.

'You two were inseparable,' Lucy teased, her eyes dancing with amusement. 'And he was quite the catch, if I do say so myself.'

Despite my embarrassment, a bit of excitement coursed through me. The way Lucy described him—a charming smile, kind eyes, and a good laugh—it made my heart flutter. Maybe, just maybe, I had met someone special.

To add insult to injury, poor Lucy had been left to entertain his less-than-attractive mate, a fact that only added to the cringe-worthiness of the situation.

'By the way,' Lucy said with a smirk, 'I swapped numbers with them, and we all agreed to meet up again tonight.' My heart sank as the realization hit me like a ton of bricks: I was essentially walking into a blind date. Panic started to set in as I imagined the awkwardness of facing these guys again, not knowing what embarrassing antics I might have subjected myself to the night before.

'Are you serious?' I groaned, burying my face in my hands.

Lucy laughed. 'Oh, come on, it'll be fun! Besides, you really seemed to like him.'

I knew that this was definitely going to be an interesting—and potentially cringe-worthy—evening. But beneath the panic, a flicker of excitement remained. Maybe, just maybe, this blind date would turn out to be something special.

As Lucy tried to paint a picture of his appearance, I found myself struggling to envision what he might look like. Despite her efforts to reassure me that he was 'definitely my type,' with his dark looks, DJ profession, and quirky coolness, I couldn't shake the feeling of apprehension.

'You'll love him,' Lucy insisted. 'He's got that brooding, mysterious vibe you always go for.'

While Lucy's enthusiasm was infectious, I couldn't help but wonder if reality would live up to her descriptions. Was he really as intriguing as she made him out to be, or was this another one of those cases where beer goggles had worked their magic?

Nevertheless, I braced myself for the upcoming encounter, hoping that Lucy's assurances would prove true. It was going to be an interesting night, and I could only hope that it would lean more towards exciting than cringe-worthy.

Later that evening, we made our way down to the pub. I was nervous, but the several glasses of wine had helped warm me up and give me a false sense of confidence. As we arrived, it looked like we were the first ones there. We ordered drinks and found a table, trying to settle in while we waited.

As time passed, they still hadn't shown up. By now, we were on our second, maybe third drink. Any inhibitions or apprehensions I had were quickly fading, replaced by a growing sense of anticipation and a bit of tipsy bravado.

'Maybe they chickened out,' Lucy joked, taking a sip of her drink.

'Or maybe we got the time wrong,' I suggested, trying to mask my nerves with a laugh.

Just then, the door swung open, and I saw two figures enter the pub. My heart skipped a beat, and I held my breath, hoping that the night would live up to Lucy's enthusiastic descriptions.

As I sat there, unsure of who to expect, Lucy suddenly spotted them entering the bar. 'There they are!' she whispered excitedly.

I turned my head quickly in their direction, and BOOM there he was—my blind date. I was taken aback, to say the least. This was not at all what I had imagined. I had been hoping for tall, dark, and handsome—a stereotype.

Fair play to Lucy she had had mentioned dark and quirky, but she had wisely made no promises about handsome. I'd let my own brain conjure up that illusion.

Instead of the tall, dark and handsome figure I had in my daydreams all afternoon, but what stood before me was a teeny tiny guy with the most enormous ears. He reminded me instantly of Spock from Star Trek. Beside him, his friend a totally different kettle of fictional characters—a broad, solidly built guy giving off a Shrek-like vibe (though thankfully not green).

I glanced at Lucy, who was trying not to laugh at my stunned expression. 'You said he was quirky I suppose,' I managed to say, my mind racing to adjust to the reality before me. This was definitely not what I had envisioned for my blind-date.

Observing them, I couldn't help but feel a sense of disbelief. They truly made an odd pair, and the shock must have been evident on my face because I turned to Lucy with wide eyes, silently mouthing 'OH MY GOD.' Lucy, clearing remembering them from the night before, seemed far more composed, quietly giggling at my reaction, finding the situation amusing.

Despite the initial surprise, when they offered to buy us drinks, we accepted without hesitation. Perhaps, I thought optimistically, they might start to look better after a few more drinks. With that hopeful thought in mind, we decided to stick around, eager to see how the evening would unfold. The unpredictability of blind dates often led to surprising outcomes, and I was willing to give it a chance, hoping that lurking beyond their Shrek and Spok appearances could be personalities that would charm and surprise us.

After a couple of drinks, Shrek and Spok asked us if they wanted to go back to their flat. They had only now decided to tell us they were having a party back at theirs and had snuck out to meet us. Of course, we agreed.

As we made our way to their flat, which was practically next door to the pub for the party, we found a small group of people already there, enjoying drinks and some spliffs. Spock, being a DJ, took charge of the music, showcasing his skills on the turntables with a selection of fantastic hip hop classics.

Despite my earlier reservations about him, I couldn't deny that he was actually very good at what he did. His passion for music was evident in the way he effortlessly mixed tracks and kept everyone there enjoying the beat. The atmosphere was lively, and Spock's music was an unexpected but welcomed energy to the gathering. As I watched him work the turntables, I began to appreciate his talent and understood why Lucy had described him as quirky.

As the night wore on and we indulged in a few more drinks, I found myself slipping back into the beer goggles mentality I had worn the night before. In my slightly intoxicated state, I started to see Spock in a different light and began to like him again, thinking he was 'the love of my life'. Only for him to also interpret my renewed interest, for a second night running, as a sign of mutual attraction. We were glued to one another's side, whilst the rest of the party were smoking weed in the kitchen.

Whilst everyone was distracted Shrek took the opportunity to invite Lucy to his bedroom under the guise of wanting to share some music with her. Though I sensed her reluctance, Lucy was the type to handle herself well in any situation.

Despite any reservations she may have had, she likely wanted to give me some space whilst I found myself once again falling prey to my beer goggles-induced infatuation, leaving me with Spok and becoming all 'hearty eyes' again.

Unbeknownst to me, whilst Lucy was in the room, Shrek made his move on her. She described sitting on the edge of the bed, maintaining a safe distance, while he played her some tunes. Nodding along and pretending to be entertained by his music, she found herself suddenly caught off guard when he abruptly swooped in for a kiss.

Recoiling in horror, Lucy instinctively pulled back, her body language clearly expressing discomfort. Unfortunately, Shrek persisted, continuing to lean in.

It wasn't until Lucy practically leaned her head back to a horizontal position and lowering her body swiftly backwards, creating a double-chin effect, that he finally stopped. She wasn't sure if it was the sight of a forced double chin that put him off, or that he finally got the hint and realised she was not interested.

He took it well on the surface, but Lucy couldn't help but wonder if his pride was hurt deep down. Being drunk Lucy didn't dwell on the uncomfortable situation and chose not to make a scene about it.

They rejoined us in the living room a bit later, where we were all dancing and enjoying the music. Suddenly, out of nowhere, Shrek appeared with an empty wine bottle and started rapping into it as if it were a microphone. In our merry state at the time, we thought this was amazing!

Shrek started passing the wine bottle around, and one by one, we all took turns rapping or singing into it. I couldn't tell you what nonsense I spouted into that makeshift microphone amidst the haze of tequila and blurred memories.

However, one moment stood out vividly: when the spotlight landed on Lucy. She transformed into a whole new persona, channelling the energy of Olivia Newton-John herself, attempting some wobbly voice thing as if she were on a talent show. It was quite embarrassing, to be honest.

I was completely embarrassed for her, and I was drunk with no inhibitions, anything usually goes but not in that instance.

Lucy had taken singing lessons in her younger years, and I believe this was her way of showcasing her talents to a crowd that may not have been entirely impressed with her song choice.

Nevertheless, we left the party content, singing our way up Stoke Newington High Street at 3 o'clock in the morning. It felt like we had made some newfound friends, and I couldn't shake the feeling that I had met the love of my life. Life was looking very promising in that moment.

A few days had passed, and we hadn't heard from either one of them. I was gutted. I had also borrowed Lucy's favourite cardigan that night and in my drunken state had left it there.

After a few drinks at the Three Crowns pub the following weekend, we mustered the courage to knock on their door and get the cardigan back. Most people would text them and arrange to get it back, but after a few drinks we decided this was the best option.

It took multiple attempts before they finally answered. When they did answer, their demeanour was cold and uninterested. Perhaps they felt rejected, or Lucy killed any sort of 'cool-status' when she sang into the wine bottle —who knows?

Despite their demeanour, we were still open to maintaining a friendly relationship. Without engaging in any conversation, they practically shoved the cardigan into our hands before swiftly closing the door. It was a brief and awkward encounter that left us feeling dismissed and unwelcome. To be honest, it felt quite rude, especially considering they had enjoyed our company for two nights in a row.

So, in retaliation for their rudeness, whenever we were out drinking in Stokey over the following few weeks, we played knock door run. We'd bang loudly on their door, ring the buzzer, and then hysterically run off before they could answer.

Lucy even captured photographic evidence of me cocking my leg up as we fled. Looking back, it was admittedly childish, but at the time, it felt like fitting retaliation for their dismissive behaviour. They deserved it.

I bet they wished they hadn't crossed paths with us and our drunken immaturity.

Manners had been ingrained in Lucy and me from a young age. We were taught to be polite and respectful, regardless of the situation. As adults, we upheld this principle and had little tolerance for the kind of rudeness displayed by men like them.

This was especially true when we were out drinking, letting loose and reducing ourselves to a playful and harmless form of retaliation. It was our way of asserting ourselves without stooping to their level of disrespect.

We refused to let it go, we did it more for the amusement of the situation. No fucks given. Not for them anyway.

Strangely enough, we never saw them again, even though we frequented the same pub and lived just a stone's throw away. Perhaps they moved out, or maybe they purposely kept their distance to avoid running into us again. Who knows, and frankly, who cares? We had a laugh, and that's what mattered most to us at that point in our lives.

Chapter Seventeen

The Big Election

May 2010

LUCY

There was a big general election, where no single party secured an overall majority. It was the first time since World War II that the UK faced such a coalition.

It was all everyone at work was talking about, besides what we were having for dinner that evening and what everyone was up to that weekend.

Layla and I of course had voted. But, with the incentive we would vote in the West-end and get pissed after we had placed our votes.

After a great night, we got the 73-bus home and on the back seats someone had left two masks of David Cameron and Nick Clegg.

Being tipsy, we decided to wear them on the bus ride home and poke our heads up to the bus windows and wave like we were royalty to passersby. We gave people a giggle, which spurred us on.

It got the bus in high-spirits, and I ended up chatting to a guy called Daniel, we swopped numbers and agreed to go on a date.

I'd been chatting with Daniel for two weeks before we went on a date.

We swapped social media accounts, talked on the phone at least twice a day, and text constantly. There's no doubt we got along really well.

He was gorgeous, with deep brown eyes, and a brilliant personality.

Daniel called me the morning of our date, and we excitedly spoke about how we couldn't wait to see each other again. He mentioned he didn't want to go to a pub because he'd want to eat, and he didn't trust pub food. What on earth! Alarm bells should have been ringing, but they weren't.

We decided to meet at a small Thai restaurant in Hecknell Green, which had a bar downstairs and a Thai restaurant upstairs.

FLATMATES AND BAD DATES

I figured it wouldn't be too busy because it was the weekend before payday.

We agreed to meet at 7:30 pm. It was a Friday night, and I was debating whether to drink alcohol. I had £40 to my name until the following Tuesday, and I needed to be able to afford to get to work and to buy my cod cakes and peas. I decided not to drink.

I slipped into my trusty black dress. It was usually a winner and made me look a dress size smaller. It was a black cape wrap dress that cost about £15 but it looked much more expensive. It was midi-length with a slit up the leg to show off my pins.

I left the flat and got the bus to Hecknell Green. The pub was a 10-minute walk from the bus stop and already I regretted wearing the 4.5-inch nude court shoes on my feet. I must have looked like I'd pooped myself!

I arrived and he wasn't there yet, so I texted him to let him know I'd wait inside.

We had agreed beforehand (my idea) that whoever arrived first would get the drinks in, because that initial awkward moment of saying hello and deciding what to drink can be so uncomfortable. Do I fake reaching for my wallet and hope he pays? Too awkward! I tottered into the softly lit ambiance of the pub.

I ordered a J-20 for him and a lime and soda water for myself. There was a group of lads sitting at the front of the bar, and they were staring at me (I hoped it was because I looked stunning and not like a hooker scouting for clients).

Either way, it was uncomfortable, so I opted for a table at the back where there were hardly any people. Perfect. I asked for a tray to carry the drinks over, trying not to trip in the stilts that I was wearing.

Once seated, I got comfy and retrieved my phone from my bag to make myself look occupied and not too eager. Just then, I received a text from Daniel: 'hey babes, I'm almost there, see you in a minute.' I glanced up and spotted him walking towards me.

There was definitely a mutual attraction between us. He was sitting across from me and asked if he could move to the chair next to me.

The conversation flowed effortlessly, punctuated by laughter, and the pub's calm ambiance added to the pleasant atmosphere. Whilst laughing, I playfully patted his hard, muscular leg, which only increased my attraction to him.

His phone interrupted our moment, and he mentioned he needed to go outside to take the call. I couldn't help but wonder if he was taking a fake 'emergency' call, and he was doing a runner.

Nonetheless, I decided not to panic and that I'd wait for him. After what felt like 10 minutes, he returned.

'I'm hungry, do you mind if I grab some food?' he asked. It's 9:30 pm at this point, and I felt a bit miffed, but

I agreed. I wasn't hungry myself; I had already eaten a salt and vinegar crisp sandwich before heading out. We made our way upstairs to the restaurant and found a table.

A petite waitress approached us and mentioned that the restaurant was shutting at 10pm and asked for our drink orders. He ordered tap water, and whilst laughing his head off he claimed he was on a budget.

The waitress didn't quite catch his humour, but I chuckled politely. I ordered another lime and soda water. Whilst the waitress prepared our drinks, he looked at the food menu and then pulled a disgusted look on his face.

'I'm really put off,' he remarked. I enquired why, and he pointed to a pork belly dish at the top of the menu.

I thought to myself, oh for goodness' sake, not everyone dislikes pork. How ridiculous!

He then ordered a starter of king prawns.

When they arrived within five minutes, Daniel took one bite and, with another disgusted look, said, 'They aren't very nice, and I don't like that they came out so quickly.' I gave a half-smile.

He was coming across as very fussy.

Realizing I wasn't impressed, he said, 'I'll stop moaning soon. I don't usually complain this much.'

At this point, I was thinking, yeah right, and started to wonder if I could really get along with him. He was far too critical and nit-picky. Life is far too short.

He ate some of the prawns and left one on his plate.

The waitress came back over, looking to clear the table. 'Have you finished?' she asked.

With an annoyed look on his face, he responded with a stern tone, 'I'm not finished yet.' The waitress scurried off.

He looked at me and said, 'They obviously want to get rid of us.' He then didn't even look at the prawn, proceeding to ignore it.

I said, 'Are you going to eat it?' He replied, 'Yes.' I'm thinking, 'Well, eat the fucking prawn then!'

A waiter came over five minutes later and said, 'We are shutting the kitchen soon, have you finished?' Daniel barked, 'I haven't finished yet.'

If he could snap over a prawn, what else does he get cross about that's so petty?

Eventually, he eats the goddamn prawn. It's 10:10 PM.

He finally asked for the bill.

The waitress brought it over immediately. It was obvious they were rushing to shut the restaurant, which was fair enough; it was a Friday evening, and people would have wanted to get home, not to be stuck working because of an awkward customer.

Daniel was scanning the smallest white paper bill I'd ever seen, inspecting it like a crossword puzzle with missing clues and with a puzzled look on his face, he says,

'They've put a service charge on my bill. Does this look right to you?'

He handed me the bill: Prawns £5.95, water £0.00, lime and soda £1.80. Total price £7.75. There was no service charge on there—what the fuck was he on about?

I was starting to get the feeling he wanted me to say something about paying for my drink.

If that was the case, how cheeky. I bought him a J-20 earlier, and he hadn't bought me a drink all evening.

I looked at him and said, 'There's nothing wrong with this bill; I don't know what you are on about.'

He replied in a flippant manner, 'Oh well. It's only £8 anyway.'

He rummaged around in his pockets, pulled out some change, and counted it. Obviously realizing he hadn't got enough small coins to make the £7.75, he pulled out a £20 note.

But instead of putting the £20 on the dish provided, he waits for the waitress to come over and was folding and scrunching up the £20 note up in his hands as though he was about to make some impressive origami flamingo or something with it.

He was holding onto that £20 tight, and it unnerved me. The atmosphere felt weird.

As the waitress made her move over, Daniel leaned over to me and said, 'Don't you need to go to the toilet?' I said, 'Yes,' and I got up to walk downstairs.

I did need the toilet, but it was weird that he ushered me off to the toilet without me even mentioning it. It felt like he wanted me out of sight so I wouldn't see him paying the bill. Why did he want me out of the way? I thought it was really odd, but I couldn't figure out why.

As I got down the stairs, I looked up at the restaurant and I could see him standing by the till. He saw me gawping at him, and I quickly looked away.

I went to the toilet and then waited for him by the exit of the bar since I could no longer see him and assumed he was in the men's toilets.

He came back out of the toilets minutes later, looking lighter, less agitated and happy and the weirdness that just happened upstairs in the restaurant melted away for just a moment.

We walked outside. His mood had shifted, and we were smiling and giggling about a previous date he had with someone who couldn't walk in her heels. We talked about how cold it had become, both of us doing an exaggerated shiver and giggling.

As we were about to depart ways, we hugged for about five minutes. 'I could stay here all day,' he said as he pulled me in for a peck on the lips. I jokingly respond, 'Is this allowed on a first date?' He said, 'Yes,' and pulled me back in for another kiss.

I got back to the flat and over a bottle of wine Layla and I agreed that the date was weird. I needed a second opinion, cos he was so gorgeous, I needed to know whether I was the only one that thought this bloke was strange and that he was too bad mannered to ever go on another date with.

I was hoping Layla would say that this was completely normal behaviour, but of course she did not, and I knew it wasn't either. The guy had issues deeper than I would be able to handle. Besides his rudeness would be going completely against the values I had been brought up with. So, I knew that it would never have worked out. I would have been wasting my time if I had seen him again.

It was clear to me that whatever chemistry we shared, and no matter how gorgeous he was, there were too many red flags for this to go any further. Unlike the May 2010 elections, there was no coalition, it was clear Daniel had not secured himself a seat at my table and hopefully not at this restaurants table ever again. For the waitress's sake.

Chapter Eighteen

Big Jacket

▮ LUCY

I had recently been messaging a guy named Chris on Plenty of Fish. He owned a gym in Fulham and seemed 'normal' enough to arrange a date with. Layla and I nicknamed him Pump-it Pete, thanks to the well-defined muscles bulging through his sleeves in his photos. This playful nickname made him stand out from the rest of the guys we were chatting with and added a touch of humour to what, given my dating history, could potentially be a disastrous date.

Before meeting him, I would clown around in the flat with Layla, belting out 'Pump It' by the Black-Eyed

Peas whilst dry humping the air, pretending I was shagging him. It was funny at the time.

After weeks of exchanging messages and phone calls with Pump-it Pete, the much-anticipated date had finally arrived. I suggested that we go to the restaurant on the high street up the road from mine and Layla's flat—my favourite Thai place called Yum Yums, known for its excellent cocktails and food.

It had the perfect ambience: classy and dimly lit, ideal for concealing any imperfections. The low lighting had the potential to make me look more attractive than in broad daylight. Bonus.

I decided to curl my hair with hair straighteners. Big mistake. It turned out awful, but he was already on his way from Fulham in South London. With no time to re-wash and start over, I did my best to straighten and style it, but instead of looking like a polished goddess, I ended up resembling Frizzy Lizzy from the eighties making a comeback.

I felt like crying. I was worried that he was probably going to think I was a catfish. However, he seemed like a nice person over the phone, not shallow and I thought I could at least gain a friend out of the date if nothing else.

I slipped into my blue wrap dress, a bargain I had found at the local charity shop and teamed it with some cute shiny nude court shoes.

Layla was out with her work colleagues in Camden, so I couldn't seek her opinion on my outfit.

A text message popped through.

I'm here xx

It was time to pull that confidence out of the bag, run down the flat stairs and open the door to meet what could have been my next boyfriend, or even the love of my life. Frizzy Lizzy was officially leaving the building, and a combination of nerves and excitement washed over me.

As the door slammed behind me, the high street was buzzing as usual, and Pump-it Pete was stood outside of Sainsbury's Local waiting for me. He spotted me and smiled; he had a gorgeous, friendly smile, but I was very sure he wasn't 6ft like he said he was. But my goodness there was something about him.

As he walked on over, I felt at peace already. He had a friendly warmth about him. He greeted me with a hug and his... oh hellooooo extremely muscular arms ooh lala. I reminded myself to keep my mind out of the gutter; after all, I am a lady.

As we walked on over to the restaurant and he grabbed my hand. My initial reaction was to pull it away. But I didn't want to give him mixed signals, so I went with it.

We entered the restaurant, and I felt proud that I lived in such a quirky and vibrant Borough that I was introducing him to. He ordered a table. He sounded very mature and polite for a 25-year-old. Just the type of man I was after.

We got asked if we wanted to sit at the tables on the floor where we take our shoes off. But we decided to sit at a standard table and keep our shoes on. Thank goodness, cos when I take these 4-inch heels off I instantly looked dumpier.

The conversation flowed effortlessly. He told me about his childhood, sharing stories of growing up in Nigeria under the care of his grandmother before moving to the UK to live with his mother, after his grandmother sadly passed away.

His journey fascinated me, and in comparison, my life felt like it had been very easy. I was grateful for that, very grateful and I could see why he acted very grown-up for his age.

I listened on intently, genuinely engaged for once. My eyes didn't glaze over in boredom like it usually would on a date, nor did my mind wander to trivial matters like outfit choices for the following evening's night out.

Up until then, I'd never met someone as ambitious as him, not in the form of a potential boyfriend anyway. Despite facing setbacks like an injury that ended his fulltime sports career, he used his resources wisely to establish a successful fitness business. His dedication, working seven days a week, and his aspirations for his business left me thoroughly impressed.

Could this man be any more perfect for me? He was ambitious, attentive, and driven and plus I fancied him like mad.

After dinner, we headed to the bar area where I indulged in cocktails while he opted for lemonade. He insisted on paying for everything, which was really generous of him. Especially as the bill couldn't have been cheap. I'd had a lot of cocktails, but I could tell he wanted me to have a good time. Maybe he liked me.

As the evening unfolded, we struck up a friendship with the lovely bartender, and I couldn't shake the feeling that this would become our regular spot for future date nights. We were laughing away with one another and our new friend, and I saw how amazing Pump-it Pete was in being able to communicate so well with not only me, but others too. I was smitten.

Six hours passed in a blur of non-stop conversation, and as he walked me home, we shared a warm hug before bidding each other goodnight. With the biggest smile plastered on my face, I ascended to the flat, eagerly anticipating that first text from him once he arrived home, hoping that he felt the same way.

I hadn't heard from Layla all night, so I wasn't sure if she was home, but I really hoped she was because I couldn't wait to tell her about my date. But as I opened the flat door, it was silent. 'She must be having a good night,' I thought.

I got into my bedroom and started to take my makeup off. Midway through removing my mascara, the flat buzzer goes.

'OMG please don't tell me it's him, I now have hardly any makeup on, and he is not ready to see me like this, not just yet' I panicked.

But then I thought 'Ooh maybe he is coming to give me a goodnight kiss or something.' I quickly concocted a plan in my head to put as much makeup back on as quickly as possible.

I would have had a few minutes by the time he made his way up all the stairs to my flat. It wasn't often that someone would buzz our flat late at night, although with being situated on the high-street we sometimes got people mucking about and buzzing our flat.

So, it could have been that. I tried not to panic too much.

I lifted the flat phone by the front door and quietly said 'hello?' Silence followed. I put the phone down. The buzzer went again. I picked it up and sternly asked, 'Hello? Who is this?' I heard a whimper, and a distressed voice say, 'Lucyyyyyyyy. Let me in. I've lost EVERYTHING!'

Oh, my goodness, it was Layla. I was baffled. I quickly snapped out of feeling like life was amazing and switched into Superhero flatmate mode, sensing something was wrong. Concerned, I heard Layla trudging up the flat stairs. She knocked on the door. Why was she knocking? Where were her keys? This looked bad.

I opened the door, and standing before me was 5ft 2 Layla with a tear-stained face, looking utterly miserable and drowning in the biggest man's parka coat I had ever seen. She looked pitiful, and frankly, quite hilarious. I wanted to laugh at the sight of her.

But my concern stopped me; I knew she wouldn't take it well in that moment. I was puzzled, more so because she didn't seem bothered about the coat. Whereas I was more focused on whose jacket it was and what on earth has happened.

Layla had gone out in a small, tight black bomber jacket. Not a 6ft-plus Topman coat meant for a giant, not for someone as petite as her.

'Layla, whose coat is this?' I asked, sounding like a concerned mother. She was crying loudly, not just shedding tears but full-on sobbing. Through her tears, she shouted back at me, 'IT'S MINE!'

'No, it's not,' I insisted, my focus on the coat rather than why she was upset was clearly irritating her. She barged through to the kitchen, dramatically sliding down against the washing machine, and in between sobs, said, 'my life is a mess.'

It was a stark contrast to how she left the flat, smiling and looking forward to her night out. It wasn't uncommon for Layla to have crying episodes when drunk, but the jacket had added an unusual twist to the situation.

Realizing I needed to address the jacket later, I focused on Layla's urgent situation. She explained that she lost her bag containing her keys, wallet and passport for a work trip to Belgium happening on Monday.

No wonder she didn't care about the jacket. I reassured her that we would search for her bag the next morning.

The biggest challenge was that she couldn't retrace her steps and didn't remember how she got home. This was crucial because she would have needed some form of payment for transportation, whether it was a bus or a taxi where she might have left her bag.

In typical 'me' style, I wanted to save the day and felt very confident that we would find Layla's bag before Monday. I was determined and tried to convince her that everything would be okay the next day, and she should try not to panic.

Layla had been excited about her work trip, and I was horrified for her. I reassured her that we would drive around London in my car in the morning to look for it. The tears slowed down, and she seemed calmer.

So, I mentioned my concerns again in a calmer, less alarmed voice. 'So, Layla, whose coat is this?' She looked at me confused but still insisted it was hers.

She reached into the pocket, pulled out some headphones, and with tears streaming down her face again, she wailed, 'What are these? Whose are these? These aren't my headphones. These aren't my headphones. Oh, it's not my jacket.' And finally... she saw the light.

As I went to bed, I received a lovely message from Pump it Pete saying that he had a great night and asked if we could see each other again the following weekend. I decided not to mention the drama that happened tonight; he seemed sensible, and I wanted him to think I went to bed being good girlfriend material, maybe reading a book. And not trying to mop up my messy flat mate's mess.

It was Sunday morning, and it was time to get up and look for Layla's bag. We were on a mission. Surprisingly Layla didn't have a sore head, but I could tell that she was anxious. We had less than 24 hours to find her bag before her trip to Brussels the next day.

We started by going to Proud in Camden, where Layla had spent the majority of her night. Whilst we were there, I convinced her to return the big jacket and try to retrieve hers. Unfortunately, her jacket was no longer there, but she returned the big jacket regardless. Annoyingly, her bag wasn't there either, but this was just our first option.

Opting for plan B, Layla and I made our way to the local bus depot, her heart pounding with anxiety as she hoped against hope that her bag had been turned in.

Yet, once more, disappointment greeted her as her bag remained lost.

Feeling defeated and seeing no other resolution to this drama, Layla conceded to defeat, deciding to instead head to the familiar comfort of a pub, seeking refuge with a strong drink from the weight of her worries, if only for a moment.

The following morning, Layla arrived at her workplace, dragging her suitcase behind her, her mind set on a spontaneous trip to Brussels despite lacking a passport. She couldn't quite fathom the consequences of attempting to enter another country without proper documentation, but Layla was adept at dodging reality, preferring to bury herself in denial.

Most individuals would have promptly informed their boss about their inability to embark on the crucial business trip to Brussels due to lacking a passport.

However, Layla, not quite grasping reality, proceeded with her plans anyway. She was determined to shield her boss from the weekend's dramatic events, maintaining an aura of professionalism and the facade that her life was impeccably 'together,' despite the turmoil brewing behind the scenes and the reality of her situation.

She was leaving for Brussels that afternoon, she didn't have long to either come clean or find her lost bag.

Thank the lord though, because fortune smiled upon Layla that morning when a taxi company contacted her, informing her that they had retrieved her misplaced bag. A business card nestled within the bag with her work details, prompting the kind driver to return it to her at the office.

With her belongings restored, Layla was able to embark on her journey to Brussels, a sense of relief washing over her that she was able to 'save face' without letting her boss learn of the truth that unfolded the weekend before.

Layla may find herself in bother at many a times, but luck is usually on her side, and disasters all end up falling into place for her in the end. She later told me that she was going to 'wing it' and travel with her boss to the Eurostar, only to pretend before check-in that she couldn't find her passport. Layla not being the best actress, I was relieved for her sake that this plan did not go-ahead.

Chapter Nineteen

Fart Test and Food Poisoning

LUCY

After two months of dating Pump-it Pete, I had maintained my stance of not letting him stay over, and it felt like I'd played the role of a prim and proper 'lady' long enough.

I daydreamed daily about a future with Pump-it Pete—envisioning us exchanging vows on our wedding day, raising children, settling into our dream home, and even having a sausage dog named Lincoln.

The prospect of building a life together filled me with so much happiness. Naturally, I kept those thoughts and dreams to myself, afraid that sharing them might have made me seem like a desperate woman trying to trap him in a web of long-lasting commitment.

The last thing I wanted was for him to see me as some love-struck lunatic, desperately trying to fast-track our relationship to fit my fantasies. So, I played it cool.

When Pump-it Pete arrived at the flat, he casually dropped his effortlessly cool sports bag, containing his overnight essentials. He looked so fit. Together, we set off in his car for something to eat, his impeccable style and charm never failed to impress me. With excitement coursing through me, I was determined for the night to unfold flawlessly. Now that I had made the decision to invite him into my world, or rather, my flat, I was eager for everything to be just right.

Instead of dining at our usual haunt at Yum Yums' restaurant, we decided to change things up a bit and go to a Turkish restaurant in the neighbouring borough, Ashford Grove.

I had never had Turkish food before, but Layla had been here many times and told me how lovely the food was. As we stepped inside, the cozy ambiance hit me, the space alive with the chatter of families, couples, and a spirited group of ladies celebrating some special occasion.

They looked pissed (good for them). The friendly staff bustled about, keeping their professionalism amongst the busy restaurant. The smell of the food was beautiful with the aroma of spices and a barbecue smell.

The restaurant had an open kitchen, so we could see the Chefs cooking the food and working their magic.

I ordered a chicken shish kebab, with rice. What I loved most was it came out on the table with Turkish Ezme as a condiment and some flatbread.

Pump-it Pete ordered a lamb shish kebab. It smelled amazing. Of course I had wine with my dinner, but Pump-it Pete again only had lemonade. Amongst many things I liked about him, was that he didn't mind me getting tipsy and had spent the last two months driving me around whilst I enjoyed wine, and he was stone-cold sober.

This was a match made in heaven. My very own personal hot chauffeur. And he always paid for the meal. I always insisted and pretended to get out my wallet to pay when the bill arrived, but he always ushered me to put it away. Which was a good thing, as my card would have probably declined anyway.

Pump-it Pete had a presence about him, which made him stand out and this often got us chatting to strangers. He was polite and I felt very proud to be standing next to him. I hoped he felt the same about me. He dressed extremely classy, and always looked really smart and well put together.

After a really good dinner, we headed back to the flat. Layla was away at her friend's house in St. Albans for the weekend, so we had the flat to ourselves. Initially it was nice we could spend time for our first full night together alone.

As the evening drew to a close, Pump-it Pete and I retreated to bed, shedding our evening clothes for comfort. He undressed to his boxers whilst I slipped into a silky slip chemise.

Nestled together, we cozied up under the covers, ready to lose ourselves in the world of a film. Wrapped in each other's arms, the night unfolds exactly as I had imagined.

'I could be with this man forever,' I thought. With a contented sigh, I found myself, feeling completely at peace in his presence.

I couldn't be happier, and I was as happy as a pig in shit. We fell asleep.

As the first light of dawn filtered through the window and the cheerful chirping of birds filled the air, I was abruptly awoken by the pain of uncontrollable gurgling in my stomach. Being half-asleep, it took me a little while to fully grasp what was happening, but it soon became clear that all was not well. Glancing at the clock, I groaned inwardly to see that it was a painfully early 5 a.m.

A wave of nausea washed over me, threatening to disrupt the happiness I had imagined for our first morning together. I lay there, torn between the desire to cling to the peacefulness of the morning and the urgent call of my unsettled stomach.

In my daydreams of this very moment, I had imagined a calm and romantic wake-up, complete with cuddles and lazy moments spent in bed with Pump-it Pete, before heading out for a leisurely breakfast together.

But reality intervened, and the relentless onslaught of stomach gurgles and the desperate need to use the toilet left me with no choice but to abandon my idyllic plans.

With a reluctant sigh, I slipped out of bed, careful not to disturb Pump-it Pete from his sleep, and hastily made my way down the corridor in search of relief in the bathroom.

As I sat on the toilet, the only way I could describe it was like a trumpet blasting through the room, followed by a mix of gurgles and splashes that would have impressed an entire orchestra.

I was very aware that Pump-it Pete had probably woken up by now after the loud noises and the twenty flushes of the toilet. I was so, so embarrassed. I wanted to fall down the toilet and never come back out.

I then proceeded to be sick in the bath right next to the toilet; it couldn't have got any worse. My smug state of happiness from last night didn't last long, and I was mortified. I couldn't get off the toilet. It wasn't stopping, and I couldn't stop being sick. It dawned on me that I indeed had food poisoning. I had never had it before. My hair was dripping with sweat; I must have looked awful.

To intensify this unfolding drama, our crappy (no pun intended) toilet chose at that moment to clog up. With dread pooling in my stomach, I was left with no alternative but to halt the shit brigade and confront the problem head-on. I needed to get a coat hanger from my bedroom, where Pump-it Pete was meant to be sleeping, to try to unblock the toilet.

Bracing myself, I quietly navigated the corridor towards my bedroom, feeling the weight of every step like a march to my own personal execution.

As I did the walk of shame down the corridor, hoping and praying I didn't shit myself, I feared that the tiny flat now stank, and the absence of air freshener added another layer of distress to this embarrassing situation.

I heard movement. FUCK. He was awake. I was mortified.

Layla and I had never splurged on Andrex toilet roll; instead, we always bought four rolls for a pound from some independent cheap shop on the high street. It wasn't quite like wiping your arse with tracing paper, like those rolls that they had at school, but it was definitely rougher than the soft luxury of Andrex. After all that wiping, my arse felt like it had been through a cheese grater. Every step across the hallway was a new adventure in agony.

How was I supposed to look upbeat when I was walking like I had a pineapple stuck up my backside?

Entering the bedroom, there he was, gleaming at me, looking all gorgeous with a big grin. He said, 'Good morning.' I lowered my head and very quietly muttered, 'Good morning. I don't feel well.'

Highly aware of my sweaty face and dripping wet hair, I could only imagine how he must have been looking at me in that new light.

I knew that he and I were too good to be true.

I was internalizing feelings of anger towards that delicious Turkish food right then. Aware of how aloof I was being and still hopeful I could disguise the issue, but my face told a different story as I went bright red, something I hadn't done since school.

I opened my wardrobe, grabbed a coat hanger, and scurried out of the bedroom.

I just knew. He knew.

I walked into the bathroom and shut the door behind me, ready to get to work on ramming the coat hanger down the toilet.

Seconds later, Pump-it Pete knocked on the door, concerned, asking if I was okay. Could this be any more embarrassing?

I wanted to ask him to leave, but I didn't want him to go because I was still determined that we were going to have our 'perfect' morning together. I wished that this was a horrible dream, but it wasn't.

I stuttered back that I was okay and would be out as soon as possible, also concerned that he was probably desperate for a morning wee.

I rammed the coat hanger down the toilet as fast as I could, trying to release the blockage.

It worked.

Thank. Fuck.

And after all the stress, my stomach seemed to have settled. Phew.

I brushed my teeth and took a quick shower, washing my hair since wet hair would look way sexier than sweaty hair and it would explain why I had been in the bathroom so long.

Who was I kidding? After the warm, refreshing shower, I dried myself, towel-dried my hair, and threw my silk slip back on.

I opened the bathroom door, heart pounding and feeling completely ashamed and embarrassed, and headed back into the bedroom.

Pump-it Pete had gotten back into bed.

Finally, I knew that I could get my perfect morning back on track. I lay on Pump-it Pete's chest, and he put his arm around me. There was a peaceful silence, but I could feel the elephant in the room. He knew what had happened, but he was too polite to say anything.

Amidst my thoughts, I got a sudden strong whiff of poo.

'Weird. Maybe it just got right up my nose. It would pass,' I couldn't help but think.

It didn't pass. I looked down at my nightie and saw the evidence. Whilst frantically unblocking the toilet, it must have caused a splash back, and I had diarrhoea on my slip.

This couldn't get any worse. The lyrics from Outkast's 'Roses' began looping in my head: *'I know you like to think your shit don't stank, but lean a little closer, see roses really smell like poo-poo-ooh.'*

I didn't know what to do. All I could do was pray that he hadn't noticed the smell. Although at this point, the flat must have reeked, and I was probably delusional to think otherwise. I could smell shampoo and body wash from the shower I'd taken earlier, so hopefully, that had helped mask some of the odour. But my nose might have become accustomed to the stench after spending so much time in the bathroom.

I jumped out of bed and, in a squeaky voice, asked, 'Coffee? Would you like coffee?' Thankfully, he agreed, and I quickly grabbed some clothes from my drawers to change into whilst I made the drinks.

After I was dressed and the coffee was brewing, I headed back into the bedroom, ready to come clean about everything. It was clear he knew something was up, and not saying anything would only make me look childish. I took a deep breath and admitted it all.

He quickly confirmed he was aware of what had happened. In a very understanding tone, he tried to reassure me, 'It's only natural, babe; it has happened to us all.'

Despite his kind words, all I could think about was 'oh god am I going to become one of those legendary stories that people share around the world?'

Despite my initial fears that my mortifying morning would ruin Pump-it Pete's perception of me as someone who doesn't deal with the realities of bodily functions, his continued interest in seeing me again completely caught me off guard. I had convinced myself that this unfortunate incident would be the end of our budding romance, expecting the texts and calls to dwindle. But they didn't.

To my surprise, Pump-it Pete's view of me remained unchanged. He accepted me as I was—food poisoning and all—with a maturity and understanding that left me immensely relieved. I had feared this would shatter his idealistic view of me as someone who never poos or farts. He quickly realized that I do both.

The following weekend, Pump-it Pete came to stay again. With Layla out for the night, we decided to have a cozy evening in with a Chinese takeaway and a film. He brought over the DVD of *Obsessed*, featuring Idris Elba and Beyoncé. When he mentioned that I reminded him of the psycho blonde in the film, I just hoped that this was banter and laughed it off.

As we settled onto the small two-seater cream faux leather sofa and tucked into our Chinese takeaway, I felt a surge of happiness and satisfaction. I had fallen even deeper for Pump-it Pete and felt like nothing could go wrong. He had seen the worst of me, and now he could only see the best of me.

When it was time for a toilet break, Pump-it Pete paused the film so I wouldn't miss anything and off I went to the bathroom. As I sat down on the toilet, a massive, loud trump escaped from beneath me, creating an echo effect in the bathroom.

I stayed on the toilet longer than necessary, frozen in shock and unable to move. I couldn't help but think he must have heard it. But maybe he didn't? I could only hope and pray he hadn't. I hadn't prayed in a long time, but there I was, sitting on the toilet cringing, with my hands clasped together, pleading with the universe that he didn't hear.

After the previous weekend's events, I feared he might think I had serious bowel issues or that this was the beginning of another episode of food poisoning. I flushed the toilet, washed my hands, and made my way back to the living room, which was right next to the bathroom.

Trying to muster some fake confidence, I forced a big grin on my face and acted as if nothing had happened as I walked over to the sofa and rested my head on his shoulder. He pressed play on the film again, and the night continued. But in the back of my mind, all I could think about was whether he had heard me trump.

We went to bed, and I heard Layla come into the flat in the early hours of the morning. I hoped she had a really good night and couldn't wait to talk to her. I knew she would make me feel better about the whole situation. She'd laugh uncontrollably, and I needed someone to add some light-hearted humour to this mortifying moment.

Pump-it Pete and I had our perfect morning. We walked to Dalston for breakfast, hand in hand, smiling and laughing. We looked like a typically happy couple with no cares in the world—except for the big fart that I couldn't get out of my head.

On that very walk, with the memory of the fart still fresh in my mind, Pump-it Pete turned to me and asked if we could be exclusive. I was over the moon, thrilled beyond belief, but mostly just... shocked. Did he not hear that monumental toot? Or maybe he did, and if he did, perhaps he was so impressed that he couldn't bear the thought of another man walking beside the lady who let rip like a foghorn.

Pump-it Pete had to get to the gym that afternoon, so after breakfast, he left, and I couldn't get back to the flat quickly enough. I ran through the flat with eagerness and found Layla in the kitchen, sitting at the table with a cup of tea.

As I recounted what had happened, a lightbulb moment hit me. The only way to know if he had heard the big trump was to go into the bathroom, shut the door, and blow some raspberry impressions from my mouth to see if Layla could hear it. We called it the 'fart test.'

And so, I did. After coming out of the bathroom, eager to know whether she had heard, Layla said, 'Yes, I heard.' I asked, 'Was it loud?' She burst into laughter, replying, 'Fucking was,' as she started laughing uncontrollably.

I then wondered if maybe I had blown the raspberry a little too loud and that perhaps he hadn't heard it because it might have been quieter. So, I went back into the bathroom, shut the door, and had Layla sit exactly where he had been sitting on the sofa.

I went through all different volumes of trumps, from very quiet (which my real trump hadn't been) to moderately loud. She heard them all.

I was doomed.

What if he was telling all his friends about this? I had already met his best mate, who was a real piss-taker type comedian with no filter. I could just imagine being the butt of all jokes.

Despite everything, we had figured out that he had definitely heard.

He was accepting me for who I was—farts and food poisoning and all. No matter how embarrassing and cringeworthy these moments were, he was staying put.

Hopefully.

I mentally decided to shake it off and hoped that one day he would forget, and I would live this down in my head. Maybe one day, when we were old and ancient and had nothing else to talk about, we would bring this moment up and be in fits of giggles together.

However, I was grateful that, despite the fart and the food poisoning being the most embarrassing moments for me, it gave Layla and me a chance to laugh so hard at the situation that I was almost, just almost, pleased it had happened—if only for the laughter.

Chapter Twenty

Dancing Queens

LAYLA

By now, we had unquestionably settled into the London way of living, embracing the work hard, play hard ethic. Most of the play hard ethic entailed going to the pub for drinks or stumbling downstairs to Sainsbury's drunk to top up on wine and grab a bag of Monster Munch. I could taste the deliciousness of the combo in my mouth now—rosé wine and pickled onion, yum.

One afternoon at work, I was sent off to a meeting in Covent Garden, and at that point I had become very familiar with the streets of the West End, so I preferred to walk rather than use the tube.

With the meeting done, I wandered back through the busy streets, having a cheeky look in some of the shops. I ended up on Langley Street, and what did I stumble across but the world-famous Pineapple Dance Studio!

With glamorous, beautiful-looking people decked out in Lycra and spandex hanging around outside—midriff tops, sweatbands—I was trying to stay cool and contain the excitement I must have been exhibiting. It felt like I'd walked onto the set of a West End musical; these people didn't look like us mere mortals but a different species altogether.

I had to compose myself and carry on past, reminding myself that I really should be back at work by now anyway.

A few hours later, sitting at my desk, I couldn't get the image of those beautiful people out of my mind. So, I decided to Google and check out the Pineapple Dance Studio website. I found the information page, and there was a link for classes—ooh, I wondered what sort of classes they had for beginners! After some scrolling, I discovered they offered everything from tap to street dance, and not just for the beautiful and talented!

I'm sure you've already guessed what I was thinking. Oh yes, Lucy and I could go and have a little dance session at Pineapple! I couldn't wait to tell her about it later!

So, that night back at the flat, over a glass of obligatory weeknight wine, I told her all about my brilliant idea, and no surprises, she was in!

I booked us on to a beginners' street dance class for that coming Friday night, and we both disappeared off to our rooms in search of something flash dance to wear, spandex is out of the question, but I was sure I had some stripey pink leggings stuffed in a drawer somewhere.

That Friday evening, we met up outside Covent Garden Tube Station. We had both already changed into our gym gear in the work toilets. I was in my stripey leggings and a baggy oversized black T-shirt, while Lucy, being Lucy, had nipped off to Topshop on her lunch break and bought a jazzy black and white leggings and T-shirt combo.

We headed over to Langley Street and walked into Pineapple. After signing in at reception, a young girl directed us to join a line of people standing outside one of the studios. There was a group just finishing up, and with the door half open, we caught a glimpse inside. Surely those dancers couldn't be beginners—the way they were throwing themselves all over the place with such precision was mesmerizing!

The class finished, and the dancers shuffled out all hot and sweaty. Lucy and I looked at each other. We walked in and found ourselves standing in a blindingly white studio with a huge mirror covering the entire wall in front of us.

These people did not look like rookies. The first feeling of doubt set in as they threw off their jumpers to reveal washboard stomachs, toned and muscly arms and legs. Some had started warming up, kicking their legs high into the air and then easily settling them onto the ballet bar, effortlessly bending over and resting their foreheads on their toes.

I looked at Lucy and she looked back at me. Telepathically, we communicated our thoughts: this was not what we had imagined. Clearly, these people were not beginners. Had I booked the wrong class, or had I seriously messed up and signed us up with the professionals?

The class teacher was a tiny little woman, probably about four foot and a fag paper, but boy, could she hold a room. She knew everybody.

I saw her eyeing us curiously. We must have stuck out like sore thumbs in the middle of this crowd, shuffling around nervously with our heads down, like the unpopular kids at a school disco. Suddenly, the room jumped to life as hip hop blasted from the speakers; it was warm-up time! Lucy and I exchanged glances—there was no going back now!

The teeny tiny teacher started shouting out instructions like a garage MC, wearing one of those Madonna headsets. She really looked the part. Everyone else in the room followed the moves in a fluid-like motion. I tried so hard to copy them, but my body was in no way cooperating. My arms and legs flailed everywhere. I caught a glimpse of myself in the mirror and was horrified by what I saw—I looked like a demented chicken.

Lucy was doing alright and had managed to pick up some of the moves. While not perfect, she could carry it off better and had her head up; she looked like she was enjoying it. I wished I could say the same!

Warm-up finished, and it was time to learn the dance routine. I had failed miserably to master a few simple steps, so I wasn't feeling optimistic. The first few moves were okay—a bit of a sidestep here, a forward, a backward, and a little twirl. A small amount of confidence crept in; maybe I had this. I was going in the same direction as the other dancers, which surely had to be a good sign.

This was repeated several times, and I was happily stuck in my repetitive bubble, lulled into a false sense of security. If only that had been it, but then she added a few more advanced moves, without stopping, shouting through her Madonna headset, and immediately I was back in crazy chicken mode. I watched in the mirror as the other dancers glided into the steps as if they were performing on a West End stage!

I had been so focused on myself that I hadn't seen how Lucy was getting on. I looked over, and the smiling, airy confidence she had shown during the warm-up had vanished. She now looked more like me, although she remained the coolest cucumber out of the two of us. I could tell by her face that she was no longer enjoying this; not so much embarrassed like me, but she looked bored.

We were given a 5-minute break, and Lucy and I guzzled down water like we hadn't had a drink in a month. We had both had enough and wanted to escape, but before we could make a run for it, Madonna called us all back to our spaces. Apparently, we were going to perform the whole routine, coming forward in rows with an individual freestyle thrown in! Oh God, no—this was it. We *had* to get out of there.

How on earth were we going to come up with a bloody freestyle when we couldn't even follow a basic warm-up? I doubted that the Macarena would go down well.

My mind was transported back to 1992 when I had a couple of mates over. I had been boasting about my dancing skills (I did tap and modern), but they didn't look convinced. I was a bit clumsy in those days, so to prove my theory, I went upstairs, put on all my Lycra gear, and came bursting through the living room door, pirouetting all the way. I ended up headfirst into my mum's rather large Swiss cheese plant.

Judging by the look on Lucy's face, which was now as white as the studio walls, she wasn't up for this either. But we were trapped, and so reluctantly, we took our places with everybody else.

The first line started to move forward for their big debut. As the third line back, we had a few minutes before we were thrust into the limelight. We looked at one another, and Lucy nodded her head towards the door, as if to suggest, 'Let's run.' Obviously, I wasn't going to protest. Not really knowing how to make an exit without being noticed, we decided to wing it, boogying our way to the back of the room, pretending we were still part of the dance routine. Maybe they might think we were just going for a swig of water?

We grabbed our stuff and, without a glance backwards, legged it from the studio. Once outside the room, we peered through the window and into the studio, and were soon in fits of giggles. The teacher hadn't even noticed us leave, or if she had, she wasn't surprised—probably more surprised that we'd lasted as long as we did. The other dancers didn't even flinch.

I wasn't sure if I should have been offended, but they clearly knew we weren't in their league, not in any league as far as dancing went. Our dreams of being part of the cool gang at Pineapple were well and truly binned. Even if we wanted to give it another go, we could never show our faces there again.

A little while later, we found our sanctuary in the pub across the road. After our dance trauma, the only remedy was an enormous glass of wine. We dumped our bags on the table and fell into our seats.

Back at the flat, the tears of laughter had almost dried up. We poured the wine, and Lucy, in a serious tone, announced, 'I did like doing something other than drinking. You love Banksy, so why don't we go around London in my car with my camera and take lots of pictures of all the Banksy art?'

Bloody brilliant idea! I had loved Banksy for years and had introduced Lucy to my passion for his art. At first, she pretended to be interested, but I knew she was just humouring me. However, since she started working with a talented artist named Nick, she seemed to have developed a genuine interest in art.

That Saturday afternoon, Lucy decided she would do us a 'pack-up' for our trip around London to look at Banksy's artwork.

I wished she hadn't, she was on one of 'her diets' again (not one that I was on board with this time). She made us a really boring tuna salad and it stunk. It was also hot weather and with the heat in her sardine sized Ford KA car, it was stinking out the vehicle. Having no air-con was actually a delight, cos all the windows were open, and I could stick my head out of the window to avoid the stench.

We went over to Bethnal Green to see the Yellow Line Flower Painter, the cash machine girl near Exmouth Market in North London and many of the famous placard rats. We were having a right giggle, although parking around London was always stressful.

When we got home, we felt a sense of achievement. I asked Lucy if I could look at the photos. As she pulled her camera from her bag and switched it on, she had a face full of panic and said, 'I don't know how to say this Layla.'

Wondering what she was on about and completely puzzled by her usual St Tropez fake tanned face turning a shade of white I asked 'Lucy, what is it?'

Lucy's eyes widened to a size I had never seen before, quite astonishing really. She said 'There are no photos on my camera. I don't know where they've gone.'

I put my hands to my head and couldn't help but laugh, even though I was absolutely gutted. Lucy wasn't laughing. I sensed she needed reassurance and with Lucy being ever the enthusiast she said, 'it's ok, we can go again tomorrow?' I had no words, but she could tell from my face it was a firm 'No.'

Lucy spent the rest of the evening, hooking her camera up to the laptop in the hope that she could retrieve the missing photos, but they were never found. Like Banksy and his unknown identity, those photos will also remain a mystery.

Chapter Twenty-One

Fireman's Lift

LUCY

After having a giggle with Layla about her Mexican birthday party one night, I suddenly developed a craving for Mexican food. Since Pump-it Pete would always take me out for dinner, I decided it was my turn to cook for him and make some beef steak burritos. Maybe this would impress him. Layla was away for the weekend, so I had the flat to myself.

I went online and found the perfect recipe. That Saturday morning, I marinated the beef steak in cumin powder, onion powder, black pepper, and cayenne pepper, letting it soak up all the flavours until Pump-it Pete came over in the evening.

It was the first time I had cooked for Pump-it Pete, and as the saying goes, 'the way to a man's heart is through his stomach,' so I knew I had to get this right.

Pump-it Pete rang the buzzer to the flat. I picked up the receiver and chirped, 'Come on in,' as I hit the buzzer to open the door.

He greeted me with a bottle of red wine and a big, cheeky grin on his face. In that moment, I just wanted to squeeze him—he was absolutely adorable. I was on cloud nine just being in his presence.

I started to fry up the beef in the frying pan, adding in some black beans and microwave rice. I then filled the tortillas and sprinkled over some cheddar cheese. I wrapped them in tin foil and popped them in the oven to crisp up the tortillas for five minutes. I served with lettuce, tomato and cucumber. They smelt amazing and looked good too.

As we both tucked in, and on first bite it was bland and disgusting. Nothing like the Mexican restaurant had served up. The steak was tougher than I could have anticipated, and we were taking ages to chew.

Pump-it Pete was struggling but pretending he was enjoying his food, even though every bite he took was taking what felt like ten minutes before he could talk again.

Instead of laughing about the situation, I just muttered 'Ooh these are lovely if I say so myself. I hope it's ok for you?'

He just nodded and said, 'Thank you for making the effort.'

For fucks sake, making the effort? It was shit and I just hoped that it didn't put him off me. But nothing could have been any worse than having food poisoning again.

It was Pump-it Pete's birthday the following weekend, he was going to be 26 and I was excited that he wanted to spend his birthday weekend celebrating with me rather than with his friends.

Not having much money, I couldn't do anything extravagant for him, but I offered to cook for him that Saturday evening, the night before his birthday. As I eagerly anticipated the upcoming celebration, I couldn't help but feel grateful for the opportunity to show Pump-it Pete just how much he meant to me, even with limited funds.

I put careful thought into selecting the perfect gifts to show him how much I cared. Despite my budgetary constraints, I was determined to make his day special. Drawing on our shared love for motivation, I purchased the book I had read in Vegas, *How to Get from Where You Are to Where You Want to Be*. As an ambitious guy, I knew he would love it.

To complement this, I stumbled upon a fantastic find—a Hugo Boss t-shirt from a sample sale, priced at a mere fiver. It was a stroke of luck that allowed me to present him with a stylish and high-quality garment without breaking the bank. And to complete the gifts, I chose a bottle of aftershave, a classic and practical gift that I knew he'd appreciate. It looked like I had spent a lot, but I hadn't. Win.

As the working week came to an end, Layla and I met up for our customary Friday evening ritual: after-work drinks in Soho. The ambiance of the bustling streets and the promise of relaxation after a long week filled me with excitement.

However, this night, the wine seemed to affect me more than usual, its intoxicating effects quickly taking hold and leaving me feeling unpleasantly light-headed. After indulging in a few more drinks in Soho, we decided to hop on a bus back to Stoke Newington, eager to continue our evening of merriment in the comfort of our flat. We stuck on the radio, drinking and dancing away.

Pump-it Pete and I were messaging throughout the night, and at around 11 pm, he sent me a goodnight message. Aww, he made me so happy.

He hadn't yet taken off his profile from Plenty of Fish, so neither had I, and I never asked him about it either, probably out of fear of scaring him off, which was ridiculous, really.

I didn't expect he would still be using it, as I wasn't, especially since he had asked me to be his girlfriend. I just used it to check if he ever logged in because it showed when someone was last online. And keeping my beady little eye on him, to test his loyalty. So far, he hadn't been online since our first date. But I obsessively checked anyway and assumed he had forgotten to take his profile off.

An hour later, as part of my daily routine I logged online to Plenty of Fish to see when he was last online, and I saw that he was also online. What the fuck!!!

Pissed, angry and suddenly without a filter I text him *'I thought you were going to sleep!!!!! Why the hell would you say goodnight to me when you weren't going to sleep? I see you are online and why are you still on a dating site anyway? You are meant to be with me! Who are you messaging?'*

As I finally took myself to bed, with anger and resentment still coursing through me, I couldn't help but hope for an apology and some clarity in the morning. The ball was in his court now, and I could only wait to see how he'd respond to my late-night outburst.

I woke up to a text message: *'How dare you send me a message like that so it's the first thing I see in the morning? Who the hell do you think you are? Do not contact me again, you bitch. I'm going solo.'*

WOWWWWWWWWWWWWWWWWWW.

I had never seen that side of Pump-it Pete before. I was shocked, hurt, and embarrassed that I had sent the drunken, somewhat possessive message. The abruptness of his decision to end things, coupled with the nasty choice of words, left me reeling.

I felt not only wounded by his rejection but also deeply angered by the manner in which he chose to address his behaviour. Instead of reassuring me and explaining himself like a respectful guy would, he had lashed out, leaving me feeling more vulnerable than ever. The birthday plans I had eagerly prepared for him now lay shattered, replaced by a bitter sense of disappointment.

Maybe he had planned this argument just to avoid having any of my cooking on his birthday? He loved good food, and perhaps he was genuinely terrified of what I might whip up next.

How could I have told him that my usual diet consisted of cod cakes, peas, and gravy, with some Monster Munch and wine thrown in for dessert? I couldn't exactly serve that to the birthday boy with his tantalizing taste buds.

Later, I saw that he had added to his Twitter account, 'I'm going solo.' He was now officially single again, I was gutted.

But despite the pain of the situation, I resolved to take a stand for myself. I refused to reach out to him, even on his birthday, as I wouldn't subject myself to further mistreatment. His dismissive attitude and hurtful words made it clear that he didn't deserve a place in my life. Still, an anxious feeling settled deep in my stomach.

I knew I needed to reshape my future daydreams, now without him in them.

Layla was going away for the weekend, but despite her own plans, she selflessly offered to stay by my side, ensuring I wouldn't have to face that difficult time alone. She certainly kept me distracted, never one to disappoint. With her boundless energy and infectious enthusiasm, she proved to be the perfect antidote to my pain, making my heartache feel just a little lighter.

After watching Sex and The City on repeat, which is fantastic for strong-women vibes and making me realise I did not need a man and would not be spoken to in such a way. I had come to learn that to get over someone you must get under someone else.

But not being one for a one-night stand I wasn't going to sleep with anyone, but I was certainly on a mission to meet someone new and swap a number or two with some randoms to get him out of my messy head.

Throughout the day, we were hungover, so I made Layla and myself some typical hangover food: pasta with a jar of tomato sauce and lots of cheese. After we were full, I tipped the leftover pasta into the bin and poured washing-up liquid over it so that neither of us, in our drunken states later, would fish it out to binge eat. Layla always found it funny that I did this, but she had also started to adopt this strategy.

For the record I had never fished out food that I have thrown into the bin, but I couldn't trust myself that this wouldn't ever happen, and I saw this tip from someone in a magazine so gave it a go once and then it became something of a habit.

Despite the horrible exchange between Pump-it Pete and me, I decided to send him the gifts I had bought before our falling out. Visiting the post office, I packaged up the presents with determination, feeling a sense of closure as I prepared to send them on their way.

Whilst our future remained uncertain and the possibility of never speaking again loomed large, a part of me still clung to the hope that our relationship could be salvaged. Yet, even if that wasn't the case, I refused to let bitterness or anger dictate my actions. These gifts were chosen with care and love, and I saw no reason why they should go to waste simply because of a disagreement. I also sent them as a reminder that I still cared despite the fallout we had.

I jumped in the shower to freshen up before Layla's and my night out. Whilst washing my hair, I decided to sing the same line repeatedly, 'I'm gonna wash that man right outta my hair,' from *South Pacific*, and frantically scrubbed my hair in the hope that this would work. But nope. I was still heartbroken, but I now also had a sore head.

Whilst Layla and I put on our makeup, we had some pre-drinks. It always made the night cheaper if we were already wasted before we went out. It was a tried and tested strategy to keep costs down, and soon enough, we found ourselves laughing and dancing away, the music pulsating through the walls of our flat.

I was surprisingly chipper, considering I had just been dumped. My mind occasionally wandered to Pump-it Pete, wondering what he was doing instead of seeing me. But the anger washed back over me, and I got my mind back in the room, laughing and having fun like I intended to do that night. Maybe he was seeing the person he was chatting to online when I caught him. The cheating bastard.

In a moment of liquid courage, I found myself wishing he could see me – carefree, confident, and without a care in the world. But even as the thought crossed my mind, I recognized it for what it was: the alcohol talking.

That night was about me and getting him out of my head, regardless of what may have just transpired.

We left the flat and headed over to the lively Three Crown's pub just off the high street, where they always had a resident DJ every Saturday evening.

Luckily, we hadn't seen Spock playing there since the night of Layla's birthday. And no sightings of Shrek, thank goodness, as I certainly didn't want to be flirting with him to try and get over Pump-it Pete.

But desperate times and all that, and if he was there, it might just happen. Maybe, just maybe, I would let him finally have that kiss he was so eager to get before. Minus the double chin.

As the night went on and we got more and more intoxicated, we started chatting with a group of men. Among them, one guy seemed particularly interested in striking up a conversation with me, whilst his friend attempted to engage Layla in discussion. Although she appeared to be listening, I could tell he was boring her because her eyes were scanning the room. His friend was also quite boring and intense, but out of desperation to get over Pump-it Pete, I tried to entertain the conversation.

As time passed and I listened intently, somehow our lips locked, and we found ourselves kissing while seated at a table in the pub.

I wasn't really into this guy; he wasn't 'my type', so I pulled away subtly to avoid being obvious about my lack of interest. I smiled at him as if I was very pleased with the sloppy kiss. I wasn't.

He asked for my number, and I gave it to him anyway.

Layla was now giggling away at the bar with another man who appeared to be buying her shots. Oh shit. This could only go one way with Layla.

Although Layla seemed to be having a brilliant time, I wanted to escape from the washing machine kiss guy. I made an excuse that it looked like Layla needed me and said goodbye, promising to come and find him later. He seemed enthusiastic about me leaving, maybe I had been boring him too. Or maybe I was the sloppy kisser.

I walked over to Layla and realized she was more hammered up close than she appeared from a distance. I couldn't understand a word she was saying, and I was so hammered too that I wasn't sure she could understand me either.

I needed the toilet, and Layla headed outside, presumably for a cigarette.

Once I came out of the toilet, Layla wasn't back in the pub, so I went outside to look for her. Panic set in when I saw Layla slumped on the floor, resting against the wall of the pub with her eyes closed.

I tried to get her up, but she couldn't stand. I just knew that I needed to get Layla back to the safety of our flat.

However, the alcohol had left me unsteady on my feet as well, making it impossible for me to support Layla's weight and navigate the journey home.

Feeling overwhelmed and unsure of what to do next, I frantically scanned the area for help, hoping to find someone who could assist us in getting back home safely. Layla always knew how to take my mind off things, though in this case, I wasn't grateful for the situation she had put us in.

In a stroke of luck, the man who had been buying Layla shots at the bar appeared just when we needed him most. With a concerned expression, he asked if everything was okay, and I quickly explained our predicament. Without hesitation, he sprang into action, coming to our rescue like a knight in shining armour.

With impressive strength, he hoisted Layla over his shoulder in a fireman's lift and began to carry her down the bustling High Street.

In any other circumstance, this display might have been embarrassing, but in our current state of intoxication, none of us were in any condition to care. As we stumbled along, I was so grateful for this stranger's kindness, but not his generosity for buying Layla the shots.

After the kind shot-buyer carried Layla up the three flights of stairs to our flat and laid her down gently on her bed, I expressed my gratitude and bid him farewell.

Once the door was shut, I made my way to Layla's room with the intention of taking off her shoes and tucking her in with a blanket.

However, when I entered her room, I was met with a surprising sight. Layla wasn't lying on her bed where she had been left; instead, she was nestled in the bottom of her wardrobe, hugging a random pair of shoes tightly to her chest (not the ones she had been wearing, as those were still on her feet).

Exhausted and lacking the energy to wake her and tell her to get out of the wardrobe, I decided to leave her be and went to bed.

As I settled under the covers, I couldn't help but chuckle at what had happened. Despite the chaos of the night, I knew that this messy moment would create so much laughter the next day.

The next morning finally arrived. I woke up before Layla and went to check on her. She was still in her wardrobe, and it was the funniest thing I had seen upon waking after a night out.

I walked into the kitchen, put the kettle on, and the noise woke Layla. She stumbled into the kitchen, asking sheepishly what on earth had happened, unable to remember how we had gotten home.

So, we sat at the kitchen table, hungover, and pieced together the events from the night before.

It certainly took my mind off of Pump-it Pete, I could always rely on Layla for that. There was never a dull moment with her around.

As the day goes on, we sat around in our pjs and my phone buzzes. It was Pump-it Pete.

He had sent me a text message saying *'the one person I wanted to hear from today on my birthday was you. Thanks for not texting me.'*

I was confused. I thought me and him were done.

I was unsure what to write back, so I left it for all of ten minutes, trying to play hardball. I was not going to apologize. I eventually wrote back, wishing him a happy birthday and stating that I was respecting his wish for me not to contact him again.

And so, it seemed… this relationship perhaps wasn't quite over after all.

However, I was very aware that certain details of the night were best left unsaid—like the drunken, sloppy kiss or Layla's adventure of being carried down the street by a stranger.

Despite what had happened, I wouldn't have changed that night for anything. It was just the sort of entertainment I needed in that moment.

Chapter Twenty-Two

Bring Your Own Bottle

LUCY

A month had passed since Pump-it Pete's birthday. Although he had asked to see me again, I wasn't so enthusiastic or persistent in putting in a specific date especially after he had the audacity to call me a bitch. He also wasn't exactly being pushy, as he had only asked me once. I felt that he should have tried harder as he was the one that had the explaining to do.

I missed him, but as time had gone on, I was getting used to not seeing him consistently anymore. It was in a phase where it could be picked up again or phased out. I wasn't quite sure.

I hadn't met anyone like Pump-it Pete before, and he ticked the majority of the boxes for someone I would want to be in a relationship with. I was gutted about the drunken text message, and the message he sent back to me. I was gutted he went online on a dating site. I was gutted about it all. But then, it crossed my mind that maybe he was online to delete his profile, but I never knew the reason why because although we were talking again none of us brought up the argument again.

Eventually Pump-it Pete started messaging me less and less, I decided not to actively search for another love interest but to date anyway because what one man can't or won't do, another man will. So maybe, just maybe, I'd find someone else that I liked and could invest time in.

I needed a distraction and decided to log back onto Plenty of Fish. I got chatting to a guy called Alex. His mum was a barrister, he worked in an office (I can't remember what he did) and he seemed like a good laugh.

Date one: We went for dinner at my favourite restaurant Yum Yums on Stoke Newington High Street. He seemed nice, very good looking (much better in the flesh) but he walked with a bit of a 'gangster hop' which if that was the case, it was a bit embarrassing.

However, I wasn't sure if there was something wrong with his leg, so I didn't want to judge.

Anyway, the date had been mediocre, but he seemed keen. Times were hard in the dating pool at that moment, so it was definitely worth a second date.

Date two: We were going for dinner in Stoke Newington, and we hadn't booked anything; we were just going to see which restaurant had a table. He was out with workmates and said he would come meet me afterwards. We decided on 8:30 pm (the cutoff time for when I started getting hungry, so this was pushing it).

He texted me at 8 pm to ask if we could meet at 9:30 pm instead. I was already starving at this point. But I texted back, 'Of course.' I had two bags of crisps while waiting and eventually went to meet him off his bus, ready for 9:30 pm.

When he arrived, he had an even larger than life exaggerated 'gangster hop' that made my eyes nearly pop out of my head. He was carrying a plastic bottle that looked like it had apple juice in it. He asked if I wanted some, and I refused. I just wanted my wine.

We went to a lovely restaurant down Church Street called Shamsudeens. The waitress showed us to our table, and asked if we wanted a drink. Alex said no (which I thought was odd) and I ordered a glass of red wine.

There were two upturned wine glasses on the table, he turned one over and started pouring 'the apple juice' out of his plastic bottle into one of the glasses. I said straight away 'You can't do that', he replied 'I can do what I want.'

I was too shocked to even reply to that and gave a disapproving schoolteacher look (like I'd never done anything shocking in my life).

We ate our food, he paid, we said goodbye and that was that.

Thing is with Alex I thought we had a mutual understanding that we didn't like one another, and I forgot all about him.

Until some months later I got a phone call from a withheld number late one night. I picked up and in a very quiet whispering voice I heard 'Hi, it's Alex. I'm really sorry I haven't been in touch. I'm inside.'

Naturally, I whisper back, 'Inside where?'

He said 'In prison. I got arrested when I arrived home after our date, and someone's managed to sneak me a phone into prison. I logged onto my email and found your number. I haven't stopped thinking about you.'

Oh great (rolling my eyes).

Being naturally nosey, I was intrigued and asked him why he had been in prison. He didn't go into detail, but he mentioned it was related to some big operation he had a minor role in, involving drugs and guns. He added that it had been all over the London papers.

I politely told him I had met someone else (I lied).

Note to previous self – Never be too polite to question the dodgy walk.

Layla and I around this time had got to know a 'dodgy DVD man'. The next day, we arranged to meet up with him, so off we went to go and meet him and pick some of the latest releases to watch.

He always insisted we sat in his car to look through the DVDs, which stank of weed and he always wore a black trilby hat. He was quite a character as he was high as a kite every time that we met him. He had one of them cars where you must lift the front seat to climb into the back.

I never told Layla, but I always used to let her get in the back of the car first, so I could sit in the front. This was just in case he ever tried to murder us cos at the time I always thought I was physically stronger than Layla and in my deluded head I would be able to kick his ass if he tried anything.

It turns out he wasn't that dodgy after all. And we watched loads of films that we didn't have to go to the cinema for.

Layla and I decided to go to one of the longest running street parties in the world on the August Bank Holiday weekend and attended Notting Hill Carnival.

We had heard many stories about the lively music that filled the streets and how much fun Notting Hill carnival is. But we were yet to experience it for ourselves.

I decided to wear a white summer dress, and a denim jacket and Layla was wearing a blue dress and denim jacket. We had whistles around our necks to create some buzz for the carnival. We were dressed to impress. Or so we thought…

Once we turned up, we were greeted with the most vibrant of outfits, adorned with feathers, sequins, tassels and face paint. Layla and I on the other hand were dressed like we were going for after-work drinks. Shit.

But the atmosphere was electric, and we walked along dancing to the music and blowing our whistles.

We were probably looking more like teachers whistling for the children to come back into the playground after breaktime as opposed to two-fun-seeking individuals.

But we were having a great time. It was like stepping into another world where all problems are left behind and where everyone was united by the love of dance, music, and celebration.

We had a few drinks before we came to the carnival, but we needed more.

We found a stall selling rum punch right next to a static sound stage.

Once we were armed with a drink in hand, we started dancing getting more and more into the good vibes. I was stood right next to the biggest speaker I had ever seen. The beats were pumping through my body, weirdly making my body hurt. I had to move away.

I thought Layla and I pumped out the tunes loudly in our flat, but we really didn't. Not compared to this. This was a sensory overload.

We got chatting to many people that day. One guy in particular caught my attention, he looked really cool and chilled.

We were giving each other the eye and he was hot. I wondered, 'Was this going to be my next date, possibly boyfriend? There couldn't be a better way to meet someone – how exciting.'

But then he smiled and had no teeth. Great!

Layla got chatting to some policemen that were in really good spirits and let us wear their hats for photo opportunities. Seemed fun and silly at the time, but we must have looked right twats!

The weeks went by, and I still hadn't seen Pump-it Pete although he was still semi on the scene in the form of messages and phone calls, I heard from him on my 26th birthday, he wanted to take me out to a barbican restaurant that had just opened near him.

But I said that I would let him know when I was free. I wasn't ready to see him again yet, as I had put on half a stone and needed to lose that before meeting him. If not, I wouldn't be my confident self, and he needed to see me at my best after all the time that had passed.

So, I convinced Layla to start the cabbage soup diet with me the next day for a kick-start.

The morning after my birthday hungover from a night drinking and dancing in the flat. We weren't ready to start the cabbage soup diet as we needed salty snacks and the usual hangover food of pasta, tomato sauce and lots of grated cheese. But we prepared the cabbage soup ready to start first thing the next day.

The flat stank of old trumps from the boiled-up cabbage. But it was ok cos we just wanted to get our dream bodies in no time. There wouldn't be anything gained from not experiencing a little pain, especially discomfort in the nostrils after breathing in the trump fumes.

The next morning, we enthusiastically discussed our motivation to start the cabbage soup diet. We both took one sip, swallowed it wincing in disgust and agreed to throw the soup in the bin. The plan for quick dream body had quickly been terminated.

My love life was hanging in the air, but I was convinced that I had found Layla's perfect match for her.

Nick who I worked with, was a talented artist, easy on the eye and I couldn't help but think him and Layla would get on really well.

Nick was hosting an art gallery in East London to showcase his talents. He mentioned he needed some waitresses to hand out wine to the guests. I volunteered straight away and roped in Kerrie, who was more than happy to help. Layla unfortunately was out with work colleagues and couldn't attend.

The event was sponsored by a top wine brand and this to me felt like what London life should be like. Opportunities that I would never have had back home and meeting people I wouldn't usually meet in circles. It was inspiring.

The event was a success, and I met his parents for the first time. They were such nice people, and I imagined that they would make great mother and father in laws for Layla. I was getting excited for her.

Ross, another colleague, was a talented musician and was in a band. He invited us all to his band night in Camden a couple of weeks after the gallery. I dragged along Layla, knowing this would full well be her scene, and I suggested that this was a great opportunity for her and Nick to hit it off.

Layla agreed she would see how the night goes, but instead of pursuing Nick she pursued the wine and got totally bladdered. Dancing along to the band, throwing all sorts of weird arm in the air shapes and being totally out of beat to the music. She looked like she was hanging her washing out one minute and riding a horse in thin air the next minute.

I wasn't even embarrassed for her, cos she was loving life and looked like she was having her own little rave in her head and forgot where she was.

Nick definitely wouldn't be interested now, and I wasn't going to suggest the idea of them two again.

Pump-it Pete had text again wanting to get plans in place to see me. I decided to go with it to see if there was a chance we could get back on track. And we did.

Months passed and Pump-it Pete and I were seeing each other again at least a couple of times a week. Time with Pump-it Pete was bliss. I felt completely spoiled again by all the restaurants he took me to that I otherwise wouldn't have experienced. I loved getting dressed up for him and showing off a new outfit to try and impress him.

Instead of eating out one Friday night he asked if I would like to go to the cinema in Fulham, near where he lived. I would then stay at his place afterwards.

I had been to his place many times before, but this time his mum was staying with him for a month. I couldn't help but think, 'Maybe tonight would be the night I would finally meet his mum?' It would have shown me that he was starting to take me seriously again. 'Maybe he would even ask me to be his girlfriend once more,' I wondered.

Pump-it Pete hired out a room for us in the cinema, it had leather reclining seats and a member of staff serving us. No man had ever done anything like that for me before and I felt very well cared for. He made me feel special. It made him special how thoughtful and organised he was with our dates.

After some cheeky kisses in our own cinema room, we went to Nando's for something to eat and returned to his house. After the most perfect date I couldn't wait to top it off and meet his Mum.

As we entered the flat, I could hear her cooking away in the kitchen. He told me to go to his bedroom while he started walking towards the kitchen. I thought, 'Okay, this is weird. Why couldn't I meet his mum? Was he embarrassed by me? Was I a secret?'

This sent my head spinning. We had been seeing each other on and off a year, and I couldn't meet his mother? Something was off. My little love bubble that I was in again was starting to burst.

The next morning, I was desperate for a wee. Too scared to risk running into his mother and revealing his 'secret,' I crept across the landing as quietly as possible. I couldn't wait to get the hell out of there.

So, the night didn't go as planned, and it was an experience I had never encountered before. However, I wasn't ready to give up on Pump-it Pete. I didn't question him; instead, I continued to act as I always had - keen and naïve. I stupidly didn't want to scare him off by speaking about my concerns and where I stood in his life.

I wasn't sure if he was heading towards me being his girlfriend again, or he was just keeping me there as an option. I didn't question it, because I enjoyed him being in my life again.

Pump-it Pete's best friend, whom I had met many times while hanging out at Pump-it Pete's gym, was a bit of a player. Eventually, though, he met a woman who seemed to stick around.

One day, Pump-it Pete asked if I'd like to go on a double date with them. I accepted. 'I may not be able to meet his mother, but at least I'm able to meet his best friend's new girlfriend. That must mean something,' I thought.

The following Saturday evening we went to Nando's, and in walks his best mate with this absolute stunner—a 10/10, 5ft, size 8 brunette with porcelain skin, brown eyes, and thick natural-looking lips. I swear, next to her, I looked like a fucking Maris Piper potato. Just peel me away and chuck me in the bin.

Given that Pump-it Pete's typical type was a brunette—and his ex was a brunette—I was gutted. She would probably be his dream girl. And, of course, we had to sit directly opposite her at the table.

I could hardly bring myself to look at her, in case I started drooling. She was that beautiful. To top it off, she casually dropped that she had an identical twin! 'Oh, bloody hell, that's it. I've lost him now. Obviously, his best mate would want to set him up with his stunning girlfriend's identical twin!

Who wouldn't want to go on a date with this gorgeous, successful guy with a bloody personality?' I thought.

I was quieter than usual, but still friendly. His best mate always put me on edge anyway—he was the type to speak his mind and had absolutely no filter. And because I was always trying to impress Pump-it Pete, I had to be on guard around that joker.

Luckily, Pump-it Pete held my hand under the table. I needed that reassurance because I was so worried he would compare me to this absolute weapon of a woman.

With Pump-it-Pete holding and stroking my hand it helped me realize that even if I wasn't as stunning as this girl, he cared about me. It didn't make me feel any less self-conscious, though, and I couldn't wait for our food to arrive so I could chomp it down and get the hell out of the company of someone who would be his dream girl.

Thankfully we didn't have to double-date again. Much to my luck it turned out that dream girl was a bit of a psycho.

Months passed, and everything seemed to be going perfectly. My parents had since moved to Belper, and we took a trip from London to Belper for a weekend with my parents. We spent a day exploring Dovedale in the Peak District and capped it off with an evening at The Talbot pub, right across from the river and waterfalls in Belper. The day and evening were absolutely picture-perfect.

Pump-it-Pete hit it off with my mum and dad right from the start. He fit in so well, and I couldn't help but feel proud to bring him to their home and show him off. He even talked about how much he dreamed of leaving London behind and settling down in a place like Belper.

And just like that, *du du du du*, wedding bells started chiming in my head.

We spent an evening at the theatre watching The Lion King and spent many cosy nights in at his and mine. Pump-it-Pete also met Kerrie for the first time and she thought he was perfect for me.

Things were finally starting to look up. But just as my head drifted back into the clouds, he went AWOL once again.

Although we were still communicating there wasn't any future plans when we would see one another. He kept expressing how busy he was, and messages weren't as frequent.

So, I had no choice but to go back to having wandering eyes until he came full circle again. If he ever did. After all, he wasn't technically my boyfriend because he never asked me to be his girlfriend again and I couldn't sit around and constantly wait for him. Even though he was the one that I was holding out for.

Chapter Twenty-Three

South of the River

LUCY

My friend Ellie had recently shared that she had attended a transformative life coaching weekend course in the heart of London. She told me it had completely shifted her perspective. Ellie had always dreamed of establishing her own prestigious jewellery business but realized she had been indulging in too much partying, which distracted her from her ambitions.

Her story reminded me of the time in Vegas when I was engrossed in Jack Canfield's *'How to Get from Where You Are to Where You Want to Be.'* The book left me feeling inspired and motivated, yet upon returning to London, I failed to implement the strategies I had eagerly absorbed. It was a shame because the book made perfect sense, but my mindset held me back and instead I chose to have a lifestyle of partying instead of working on my goals.

My school reports always echoed a similar sentiment: 'Lucy has a lot of potential, if only she wouldn't get so easily distracted.' This had also become the unfortunate truth of my adult life too.

That life-changing book had been festering away at the bottom of my canvas wardrobe since I got back from Vegas.

Feeling inspired by Ellie, I pulled the book out from the depths of my wardrobe. I loved my job, but I wasn't moving forward with my career or anything in life.

Determined to make a change, I started reading the book again. Fuelled by newfound motivation, I also signed up for the life coaching course the following weekend.

Attending the workshop was a revelation. My long-held dream of writing a book became even more compelling. I had nurtured this ambition since I was 16, having my first poem published at 14, studying media and journalism and becoming a columnist. Writing was something that I enjoyed, and I knew that I needed to get the motivation to start writing again.

Working with so many talented people and their projects outside of work, was inspiring and I wanted desperately to start working on mine. This course and book illuminated the necessity of changing my habits if I was ever going to pursue what I truly wanted. I needed to stop wasting time, and in the words of Nike 'just-do-it.'

I'd tried many times to write a novel, but I would start writing, only to get distracted by life and abandon my efforts after the first chapter.

With my newfound clarity, I realized it was time to take concrete steps toward my goals, just as Ellie had done. I was looking for a new start, an exciting new plan and with work being located in Balham, I decided that a move to South London would be a great way to re-start my motivation, in a fresh place and to get out of the habit of partying every night.

I loved my life with Layla in the flat, but I had it ingrained in my head that I needed to leave North London and be closer to work and to have a quieter, cleaner lifestyle.

I couldn't muster the courage to speak to Layla face to face. Instead, I cowardly messaged her from my bedroom, too scared to come out and confront the situation.

In my anxiety, I resorted to peeing in a cup rather than go to the bathroom in case I bumped into her. I was torn because I didn't want to leave the flat, but I had already made the decision that this was what I was going to do.

Layla replied, probably baffled as to why I didn't talk to her face when we were so close, but she didn't mention it, and understandably told me that she was going to stay in Stoke Newington. I was gutted, but I understood. Stoke Newington had become home, and this was my decision made on a whim.

When I planned in my head like that, I had to make the change as soon as possible. Which meant that I often acted on decisions without fully thinking them through. Unlike most people, I found moving to a new area exhilarating rather than daunting.

I craved change and a fresh start, and at that time, it felt like the right move to make. Less partying and more working on myself would be the path forward.

I envisioned myself getting up every morning, drinking hot lemon water, and leaving the house for work with an organic fruit and vegetable smoothie in hand. Instead, most mornings found me hungover, clutching a coffee, and struggling to get through the day. Lacking any motivation beyond my job and having a laugh.

Layla began searching for another place to live in Stoke Newington. I was looking for a cheap flat to rent on my own. But then, my ex-work colleague Ellie had just broken up with her boyfriend and reached out knowing of my search and asked if I wanted to find a place to live in South London with her and her brother, as they were both looking for a new place as well.

Without thinking it through properly, I started looking at flats to share with Ellie and her brother William in Clapham.

Ellie was a vibrant, bubbly, and fun-loving blonde with an ambitious streak. We kept in touch after I left my position as an Assistant Buyer for the high-street store, often getting together socially in South London after work. William, on the other hand, was quieter and exuded an air of intelligence. Both were nice people, and I was looking forward to this new adventure with them.

We eventually found a three-bedroom flat for rent on Clapham North Street, but it wouldn't be available for another two months. Having already handed in our four-week notice for the flat in Stoke Newington, both Layla and I were temporarily without a place to move into once the contract came to an end. Layla eventually found a place to stay in Stoke Newington, while I arranged to move in with my good friend Tom in Southgate, North London, for a month until the flat was ready.

The four-week notice period flew by, as did my time living with Tom. Life in Clapham started out fun and filled with new experiences, bars, and restaurants.

And again, I had become distracted and had not been working on my goals. I was meant to have joined a writer's group in London and meet like-minded people, but nope I was too excited by my new area.

After a couple of months living with Ellie and William in Clapham, my dad received some devastating news—he had been diagnosed with cancer. I was heartbroken and became introverted, trying to make sense of it all. The only person who I felt truly understood me was Layla.

Layla felt like home, and I instantly regretted moving out. I should have fixed myself and not my environment. Layla would have been up for helping me, and like following all the odd diets with me she would have balanced out the partying lifestyle. What had I done?

Although we still met up, I missed her more than ever and felt incredibly alone. My London experience with Layla was all I knew, and the excitement of living in South London quickly wore off. Layla and I had always spent most of our spare time together, and although I did spend some time with Ellie and William, my usual high-energy self was replaced with a subdued personality and I wasn't feeling too socialble.

Most of the time I was alone. Which would have been the perfect opportunity to work on writing a book. I'd come to London with grand dreams of success, but by this point, my biggest achievement was mastering the 'fine art' of binge drinking and partying like it was my full-time job.

Layla was still there for me, always brightening my mood. She was living with two girls in Stoke Newington, in a place she dubbed Hackney Towers.

It was a rough estate where residents cemented down their plant pots to prevent them from being stolen. Despite not being my home, I loved spending time there, being back in Stoke Newington with Layla. I still could have achieved my goals there, why had I been so stupid and impulsive?

I spent as much time away from the Clapham flat as possible, often staying at Layla's place and spending time with a guy Grace called 'Frying-Pan Face' because of his oddly shaped head, which she said looked like he'd been hit over the head with a frying pan.

I met him at Bar Revolutions in Clapham when Grace visited, and we had a night out. I drunkenly snogged him that night, but my beer goggles were definitely on. He liked me, but I didn't feel the same. I spent time with him just to get out of the flat and distract myself from my sadness.

Pump-it Pete had become busy again, so I hadn't seen him for a while and living in a pokey little bedroom in Clapham heightened my sadness even more. It wasn't inspiring sitting in there and I felt so down that writing a book was the last thing on my mind. I had come to Clapham to work on my dreams, but instead I became miserable.

One Friday evening, I had been out with 'Frying Pan Face' for drinks and returned home at 2am. Ellie and William, having returned home earlier after their own night out, had put the chain on the door, assuming I was already home and asleep. I couldn't get in the door. It was a cold November night, too late to call Layla, and I had nowhere else to go.

Panicking, I frantically called Ellie and William's phones, but they were fast asleep and didn't answer. I didn't want to stay at frying pan faces house, that would give him the wrong signals and I couldn't call Pump-it Pete, cos I didn't want to give him to see me in such a drunken state. I wanted him to have the illusion I would have been tucked up in bed by now, like good wifey material. That's if he was even thinking about me at all, and what I was up to that night.

With no other options, I repeatedly pushed the door until the chain broke, allowing me to get inside. This incident intensified my sadness, making me feel even more alone. I didn't feel like I belonged in Clapham and barely recognized myself anymore.

In a symbolic gesture, the following week I dyed my once blonde hair back to brunette, the darkness mirroring my mood. Ironically, the new colour suited me better, and I realized I should have stopped bleaching my hair years before.

I then did something I never did, and I took the initiative to ask Pump-it-Pete to meet up. I thought that seeing him may cheer me up.

We arranged to meet for dinner that Saturday evening, and I was excited for him to see my new hair. He offered to take me to a Chinese restaurant in Wimbledon. When he picked me up in his car, he said, 'Wow, Lucy. You look amazing. This is the best I have ever seen you look.'

With a big grin on my face I replied, 'Thank you, although I have put on some pounds since I last saw you.' He responded, 'No, I love it, and I love your hair. You look stunning.'

Knowing Pump-it Pete also liked curves, I realized that my weight gain from my obsession with Nando's on Clapham high street had its perks beyond just pleasing my taste buds—it had enhanced my figure as well, protruding tummy and all.

We had the best night, and despite my hopes that this would be the moment he had his 'aha' moment of realization and decide to settle down with me and want my babies, it didn't happen.

The following Saturday afternoon, my Mum and Dad came to visit, and we planned a trip to see my grandma's brother, who lived in Richmond, not far from Clapham. My dad's mum passed away when I was three years old, but I still had a few vivid memories of her. I remembered visiting her in the hospital and choosing some yellow flowers to give her; my sister chose pink. I also recalled hugging her tightly before she went into the hospital.

Beyond those memories, I didn't know too much about her younger years, so I was excited to meet her brother and learn more about my grandma. My dad hadn't seen his uncle since he was a young boy, so this visit felt significant for both of us.

My parents drove down from Belper to Clapham and picked me up. My grandma's brother, now in his 80s, agreed to meet us by the station to guide us from there.

As we approached Richmond station, we saw a little red-haired man standing on a barrier in the middle of a busy road, waving his arms frantically above his head. We instantly recognized him; he bore a striking resemblance to my grandma. We beeped at him, and he enthusiastically beckoned us to follow him as he darted across the road to a street just off the station.

We followed him down the street and greeted him at his home. I was struck by his energy and vitality, especially for his age. Despite leaving Ireland when he was young, he still had a strong Irish accent. My Grandma had also lived in London until she was 15, but due to the London smog and her asthma, she was advised to move to the countryside in Herefordshire for the cleaner air and that's where she met my Grandad.

As we chatted, I mentioned that I was living on Clapham North Street. He surprised me by saying that him and my grandma often walked down that very street when they were younger. It felt surreal to think of my grandma walking the same paths I did.

He shared stories of how my grandma loved to party and when she moved away, she would often take the train back to London to join him and their other siblings for house parties. I was starting to realise where my love of partying had come from and felt sadness, that I never got to get to know my grandma better.

We stayed for a couple of hours, enjoying his stories and company. He was now alone as his wife sadly passed away years before. He said she passed away on the morning of their wedding anniversary and they were meant to be having a party in a hired hall that night.

He said, 'I still went to the party, and left her here until people came to collect her the next day.' He was saying this in a very matter of fact manner, and looking at our shocked faces then said, 'It's what she would have wanted.'

Eventually, my grandma's brother had to leave to meet his friends. As we said our goodbyes, I told him, 'Lovely to meet you. I hope you have a nice time with your friends.' He replied with a cheeky grin, 'Oh, I will,' and made a humorous gesture with his hands, implying he would drink a bucket load of alcohol.

His playful spirit and zest for life that afternoon was inspiring. I certainly hoped that I would have that same energy and fun at his age.

FLATMATES AND BAD DATES

My parents and I went for dinner on Clapham High Street before they headed home.

I missed my mum and dad terribly and seeing them again made me miss them even more. With dad being poorly, I just wanted to be with them all the time and living in London altogether was starting to wear thin on my nerves.

Rick although living back in Cambridge helped in lifting my spirits during that period and came to stay with me the following weekend in Clapham. It was a welcome change of pace when we decided to treat ourselves to dinner at the prestigious restaurant, The Ivy.

It was Ricks idea, in the hope that Rick might spot a celebrity dining there, but unfortunately for him we didn't see any. Nevertheless, the food was absolutely delicious, and it was easy to see why celebrities would hang out at such a place.

Adding to the excitement of the day, I had been gifted a voucher to record a song at a recording studio in East London. Among all my friends, Rick was the perfect person for this sort-of-thing, due to his eccentricity and willingness to let loose.

As we arrived at the studio, we were immediately struck by its impressive setup. Tucked away in the vibrant streets of East London, the outside of the studio had an unassuming exterior. Stepping inside, there was a small hallway and on the wall was a board that had pictures of a flash car, big house and holiday destinations. I was fascinated and wondered what it was, but I later realised that it must have been the studio owners vision board.

We walked through the hallway and was greeted by a spacious room with lots of vintage instruments in the corners of the room, and state-of-the-art recording equipment that we didn't even know what it did. The control room, separated by a soundproof glass window was impressive. The engineer on duty was very friendly, and it was apparent the passion he had for music in every detail of the studio.

Posters and CD albums from well-known artists who had recorded there dotted the walls. My inner child, who dreamt of becoming a professional singer, was in its element. It took me back to a time when I was younger and put together a band with my neighbours Jenny and Sally; we called ourselves Sugar. We would use my parents' cassette recorder to record ourselves singing songs from the Sunday radio top 100 countdown. Not exactly original, but we were around the age of 8.

Rick and I excitedly entered the recording session, and despite our amateur status, we were determined to make the most of this opportunity. We decided to sing Elton John and Kiki Dee's song 'Don't Go Breaking My Heart.' Rick certainly was tone-deaf, and it made for quite a comedic CD masterpiece, at least we thought so at the time.

We decided to push our 'creative boundaries' and end the recording with some well-rehearsed banter of our own, joking about how Rick doesn't look like Declan Donnelly and telling him to stop being so obsessed about it. At the time, it was hilarious, but listening back years later, it isn't funny for anyone but us. It certainly wouldn't make it to number one and definitely wouldn't be listened to in anyone's CD player unless they wanted a laugh and a cringe at our expense.

A few weeks later my sister and her wife, Luciana, had recently a baby. My gorgeous nephew Jacob, he was their little bundle of joy and had the cutest blonde curls. They were meeting some of my sister's Uni friends in London one weekend and still living in Birmingham they asked if I could babysit Jacob one Saturday evening and if they could stay at my flat.

I was ecstatic! I felt like a proper grown-up for once, but also slightly terrified because I had never looked after a baby before. Jacob was six months old. I couldn't even keep a plant alive, but I was honoured to be asked.

When they arrived in the afternoon, they dumped their bags in the flat and we took Jacob on the tube to grab some lunch in Islington. Jacob was so cute strangers were stopping to coo over him. It was a lovely day, and it was nice to spend time with my sister and Luciana.

We headed back to my flat, where they set up a portable cot in my pokey little bedroom. They put Jacob down and told me he might wake up for milk at some point, leaving a bottle in the fridge for me to heat up. Easy peasy, I started to think.

Nope. I was so paranoid when they left for their night out that I kept checking on Jacob every few minutes. Every time I did, he had rolled onto his front. I remembered reading somewhere that this was dangerous, and armed with this knowledge I kept turning him back onto his back.

I'd leave the room, come back minutes later, and he'd be on his stomach again, face down. So, I'd turn him back onto his back. This went on all evening. I couldn't believe how much hard work it was looking after a baby. You literally cannot sit down.

I questioned all the times I wished I had a baby with Pump-it Pete and how picture perfect it would be - these dream plans were fading quick.

When my sister and Luciana returned, having had a great night, I told them what had happened. My sister just laughed and said, 'He always sleeps on his front.'

I was incredibly happy with having someone that felt like home in the Clapham flat, but once my sister, Jacob and Luciana left the next day I was lonely again.

When Layla was busy, I would leave work and head to Stoke Newington, sitting alone at a bar on Church Street. I wished I still lived there, avoiding the thought of going back to Clapham.

One evening, I met Marie, a beautiful and well-dressed woman. She was waiting for her friend Annabelle, and we struck up a conversation. She noticed I was alone and invited me to join them. Which was incredibly nice.

Annabelle, a quirky dark-haired woman, soon arrived, and the three of us spent the next couple of hours giggling and putting the world to rights. We exchanged numbers and vowed to meet up again. I drove back to Clapham feeling happy with my newfound friends.

Marie, who was five years older than me, was a true ray of sunshine. Her positivity was contagious, and her friendship arrived at just the right moment when I was feeling low and lost. As a high-achiever and partner in a marketing business. Marie reintroduced me to concepts like the law of attraction, goal-setting, and positive thinking.

Along the way, I had lost my ambition, but Marie's influence expanded my mind and slowly helped me find myself again. She discovered some positive-thinking classes in Clapham, and we decided to attend them together. This seemed like a great way to shape my mind and bring clarity to my life.

One Friday evening, we arrived at a terraced house where a woman dressed in a white robe greeted us at the door. She led us through a quiet hallway, passing a room where men and women in white robes were chanting together. The atmosphere felt serene as she guided us to a room down the corridor, where we settled into small brown leather chairs.

The woman began teaching us methods to change our mindsets, reading from sheets of paper. It was enlightening at first, but a sense of unease grew. Eventually, we realized the place was actually a cult, so needless to say, we didn't return.

Despite the encounter with the cult, my interest in changing my mindset to be more positive persisted. I delved into books like *'The Secret'* and tried to focus on self-development. The once ambitious girl who had left a small market town for London had lost her way. I had lost sight of my goals and lost touch with who I was. I needed to rediscover that drive. The drive I once had when living in Market Deeping, and the drive I was meant to have found in Clapham.

But amidst this journey, doubts began to creep in. What was I even doing in London anymore?

The desire to move closer to my parents grew stronger than ever. Aware that my parents were getting older and my dad being poorly, I needed to be within close proximity to them. I needed to be near family again.

Living three hours away from Belper in Derbyshire made it incredibly challenging. I spent many weekends commuting back and forth, staying with my parents and organizing nights out in Derby with friends from Market Deeping.

Although I knew that I needed to move closer to my parents, I wasn't sure if Derbyshire was the right fit for me. With some family and friends in Manchester, I realized that moving there would bring me just 1 hour and 15 minutes away from my parents, allowing me to see them more often while also offering better opportunities for work and a social life. This became my new plan.

During this transitional period, I spent many nights out with Marie. Her beautiful house in Enfield had a wonderful, positive vibe, and her tranquil garden with a bridge over a pond of fish was truly idyllic.

Marie understood how unhappy I was and knew about my job search in Manchester. As my rental contract in Clapham was ending, Marie generously offered for me to move in with her temporarily. I gratefully accepted her offer.

Living with Marie truly transformed my mindset. She introduced me to vision boards and the concept of chasing goals. One Saturday afternoon, we sat down and created vision boards filled with our aspirations and dreams. My board mainly focused on moving to Manchester, adopting healthier eating habits, and finding a loving relationship.

In contrast, Marie's board showcased images of a fulfilling relationship, her playing the piano, and being part of a band. She proudly displayed her vision board, whilst I tucked mine away in a wardrobe, almost as if it was an embarrassing secret.

Over time, Marie in a very short space of time successfully achieved everything on her vision board. However, for me, things didn't seem to materialize. I had simply created the board, hidden it away, and hoped that the universe would work its magic.

Marie introduced me to the art of cooking from scratch, which was a revelation for me. I was amazed when she made her own Thai green curry paste from fresh ingredients, whereas I had always just bought it from a jar at the store. Marie had a beautiful herb garden, and it was inspiring to see her cut fresh herbs from the plants and incorporate them into her cooking.

With my dad being so unwell, I realized more than ever the importance of taking care of my health. I started cooking with mostly organic meat and vegetables, making a commitment to prioritize my health and well-being going forward.

Previously, I had only ever eaten to diet or budget, so this newfound interest in cooking from scratch for health, and using fresh ingredients was a whole new world for me. A world away from my nights of eating cod cakes and peas.

In addition to exploring new recipes, Marie and I also took up running and practising yoga in the back field behind her house. We found joy in spending evenings watching classic films, and law of attraction films like '*The Secret.*' Mornings became a time for meditation, sometimes guided by a meditation CD, while the air was filled with the uplifting scent of burning geranium oil. It was like living in a retreat.

Life had never felt so wholesome and healthy. It was a time for learning and I was starting to feel alive again. Although I still missed Layla an awful lot.

Chapter Twenty-Four

Crack the Whip

LAYLA

I would be lying if I said I hadn't been feeling less and less enthusiastic about my job in recent months. Not only that, but London fatigue had set in like a bad case of the flu.

The daily commute was a circus act where I was the clown, juggling tubes and buses, getting nowhere fast and I no longer had the energy for it. Each morning felt like I was in training for the Olympics—sprinting to catch a tube, wrestling for a seat, and performing more boxing ducks and dives than Anthony Joshua, just for the privilege of eventually standing under someone's armpit.

Reaching payday and then finding I was skint again a week later, with another three to go, was becoming too familiar. My money vanished into a black hole called the Oyster card and a round of drinks at the pub—maybe the odd purchase from Topshop or Zara if I was feeling crazy.

I was still living on a diet of frozen cod cakes, peas, and the occasional cheese omelette if I was lucky. No longer living with Lucy there was no cheap laughs anymore, which didn't cost a penny.

Lucy and I were both miserable, what had we done? We should have stayed together, no matter the location.

Our friendship had been more impactful than either of us had realized, and now we were both paying the price. Instead of thriving apart, we were like two fish out of water, floating around, gasping for the good old days when we once had each other.

Not living with Lucy anymore and instead with two random strangers in Stoke Newington was like some bad version of a TV social experiment.

Moving in with strangers felt weird and being handed the room on the third floor with a lock on the door—something I'd never needed with Lucy—was bloody unsettling. As time went by, I realized that this lock was as essential as my knickers in public.

One girl was completely mental, while the other was normal enough, but both didn't exactly welcome me with open arms. They had this silent solidarity thing going on.

I felt as unwanted as Teddy Ruxpin when he wasn't offered a slice of toast.

Little did my housemates know, I felt the same way. I was only there out of desperation, with no time to be choosy, or I'd be sleeping on the streets.

I didn't want to become bosom buddies either; I just wanted to survive. I longed for the days in the pokey flat with Lucy, sharing wine and dancing nights, munching on Monster Munch in our pyjamas.

I missed Lucy and the easiness of our friendship. The grass wasn't always greener; sometimes, it was just full of weirdos and locked doors.

One of my housemates was a dominatrix. I hadn't yet witnessed anything to suggest this, other than see her leave the house on the odd occasion wearing PVC knee high boots and sporting a leather mac, with fuck-knows what underneath. It was housemate number 2 that told me. I wasn't sure if it was true or not, as I didn't realise dominatrix women came in the form of a plain-looking, short blonde with jam jar glasses.

Lucy came to stay one evening mid-week, and Jam Jar Glasses came to us in the lounge on the second floor, handed us both a beer and said, 'I apologize for what you may hear. My friend Wayne is here' Lucy and I smirked across the lounge at one another, and I piped up, 'No worries, thanks for the beer.'

Jam Jar Glasses went downstairs and then came back up with this 6ft 5 broad, brown-haired manly looking thing trailing sheepishly behind her. I think I knew what was happening, and perhaps this little rumour (my other housemate told me) was true. Or maybe she had just hooked up. Who knows.

Lucy and I were sprawled on the couch, watching some mind-numbing crap on TV. I was sipping on the gifted beer while Lucy was drinking a glass of red wine (she claims beer tastes like sweaty gym socks).

The night was chilled and great to be on the sofa with my ol mucka Lucy again. It was chilled until we heard a sharp crack from upstairs, followed by a thunderous 'Get your fucking head on the floor.' Crack!

Ok so there it was, Jam Jar Glasses was having one of her sessions with 6ft 5 floor-licking Wayne. The mental image of Wayne—this towering, broad giant—being bossed around and brought to his knees by pint-sized Jam Jar Glasses was too much.

Lucy and I were in hysterics, doubled over with laughter at the thought of Wayne's long limbs and strong-man persona being reduced to a submissive state.

'Can you even imagine?' Lucy giggled, nearly spitting out her wine. 'Big ol' Wayne, the human giant, getting his ass handed to him.'

I could barely breathe from laughing, picturing the scene upstairs.

It became quite eventful living there and I affectionately named the place 'Hackey Towers', as more of a mockery cos even though there were three floors, it felt anything but that.

Wayne, who could represent a tower became obsessed with jam jar glasses and wouldn't leave her alone. She would see him here or there, for fun but I think Wayne took his ass-kicking a little too seriously.

One sunny morning, I opened up my curtains and saw some tall man dashing behind a bush at the front of the house. Wayne? Is that you Wayne? It fucking was Wayne. What the hell was he doing?

A few nights later, I found him sleeping in our back garden. What the fuck was going on?

After a few months and with life feeling quite bizarre. I walked into work one day and found a letter on my desk. It looked formal, and I was puzzled. My boss was on holiday, so I knew it hadn't come from her. Glancing around to check if anyone had noticed, I opened it. To my horror, I read the word 'redundancy' in black and white. It felt like a huge punch in the gut.

I looked around again; if anyone had noticed, they weren't showing it. Everyone was busy getting on with their work. Also, I hadn't seen a white letter on anyone else's desk. So, was it just me?

The letter, which had come from HR, but it had the Design Director's signature at the bottom, mentioned a meeting later that day. They weren't hanging around, giving me zero time to prepare.

The rest of the morning was a daze. I couldn't concentrate on work, my head spinning with the impending meeting. I was the only non-creative on a floor full of designers, so I didn't dare tell anyone what was going on. I felt embarrassed and completely alone.

My boss was on holiday, and I didn't know if she was aware of this. I had a feeling she wasn't, as we had a great relationship. She valued my role there and was quite protective, so her absence felt like being abandoned in a jungle, surrounded by designer predators with their flashy laptops and artsy coffee mugs.

I sat there, trying to look busy whilst feeling like my entire career was disintegrating away like a Hobnob left too long in a steaming cup of tea. I was the 'nob', and I was floating to the bottom, and fast.

I went upstairs for the meeting as planned. Walking into the room, I found the design director and a member from HR both smiling at me. Fake smiling, in my opinion. The fuckers. They asked me to sit down, so I did—awkwardly.

They launched into their spiel, explaining that due to a downturn in business and sales, there was a need for cutbacks. Since my role was non-design and administrative, it was no longer a priority. The work I did would be amalgamated into the design and technical teams. Clearly, there was no room for negotiation.

I found myself nodding along with what they said, too bewildered to offer any objections or fight my case.

With my world now crashing down around me, I faced some big decisions. Who should I tell first? How would I afford to stay in London now? Should I start looking for another job? The redundancy payout wasn't exactly life-changing; it would last me a month if I was careful, and I had no savings to fall back on. My head was racing.

They told me I could have the rest of the afternoon off to process everything. Clearly blindsided, I scurried out of the building and straight to Tesco, where I bought myself some booze. Then, I headed for Soho Square. Now, I know this might sound a bit sad—to be sitting there alone, drinking—but this wasn't my first solo visit to a London park with a bottle and a problem to solve.

As I sat in Soho Square, sipping from my bottle and watching the world go by, I pondered my next move. Maybe I'd call Lucy first; she always knew how to put things in perspective. And perhaps another job wasn't such a bad idea after all. Whatever lay ahead, at least I had my trusty Tesco-bought companion and a park bench to figure it out.

I sat for a while, swigging back my bottle of cheap wine, contemplating how to break the news to my friends and family, but I couldn't face it just yet. A bit tipsy from the alcohol and the warmth of the afternoon sun, I let my eyes wander over the world around me.

Soho was perfect for people-watching. I studied the random bodies hurrying to and fro, wondering where they were going, what surprises their day had brought. Had anyone else walked into work only to find their job had ceased to exist? Probably not. It felt like just me in that moment.

In those few months of living in Hackney Towers I had recently met someone online, and whilst online dating had only proved to bring disastrous dates before, this time I had been pleasantly surprised. I liked this guy; he was easy to talk to and funny. We would spend hours on the phone chatting away.

This went on for several months, but the downside was he lived up north. Eventually, he made the journey down to London, and we got on even better in person. I then took the train up there and met his family, and after that, it became a long-distance relationship quite quickly.

With redundancy coming along around the same time, I couldn't help but think if this was a sign. His own circumstances were complicated, as he had a young daughter to whom he was, of course, committed. So, although we hadn't had a serious conversation about the logistics in the long term, I knew in my heart of hearts that for the relationship to continue, I wouldn't be able to stay in London.

In the meantime, I had to woman up and face the music with my parents. So, I pulled up my big girl pants and made the dreaded phone call home. As soon as I heard my mum's gentle and familiar voice on the other end of the line, I burst into tears like a toddler who wasn't allowed a packet of Cadburys Buttons.

After what felt like a lot of blubbering, I finally managed to calm down and explain the situation. I had a close relationship with my mum; she was always there for me, so as I stammered through my explanation, I could practically hear her getting out the 'How to parent Layla Manual' to find the chapter on 'How to Deal with Your Adult Child Falling Apart Again Over the Phone.'

The most important person I had to tell after my parents was Lucy. Even though we were both living separately, we were still close, and spent a lot of time together, meeting up regularly for drinks or food. And for any drama or crisis, which was regularly with the state of our lives.

I didn't have a long notice period to work—no more than a few weeks—so I spent most of that time packing and organizing myself for the impending departure.

So, my prospective new love interest, sent me a PG Tips Monkey, which at the time, seemed like the greatest romantic gesture. Now? A tad cringe. Anyway, it added a lot of fun to our north-south long-distance romance.

One evening, as Lucy and I were gearing ourselves up for a farewell outing, we decided to take monkey along for some fun. Determined to give him the best night of his life.

We started in Chinatown, where our furry friend accompanied us to a restaurant, watching us devour a plate of noodles like we hadn't had a meal in days. From there we moved on to Covent Garden for a sophisticated glass of wine.

We then took him on a ride on a Boris bike, monkey wobbling around in the front basket while lucy and I try to navigate the busy streets of the west end.

Slightly pissed by this point, we decided to take him on his last ride, on the number 73 bus, hanging him proudly from the strap making him look like a proper seasoned commuter. There were a lot of bemused and curious looks coming from the other passengers, probably wondering why the hell two grown women were carting a stuffed monkey around like it was an actual human being.

We got some fabulous pictures of our wild night out with Monkey.

Further farewell drinks with Lucy were initially fun but sorrowful, at least until we got spectacularly pissed and ended up in a jazz bar in Dalston with Lucy trying to dance on the dance floor with a glass of red wine and spilling it everywhere. It looked like she had pissed herself from the puddle she was dancing over.

And of course, once we got back to Stoke Newington we had to play one last game of knock-door-run on Shrek and Spok's door – much to our amusement.

My leaving do with my workmates in Soho was tame but still wonderfully messy. And then, after all that was done, I was left to ponder my future and next steps. I was heading back home to live with my parents. After three years of independence—well, madness—it was going to be strange.

The day I left was surreal. Up until that point, even though it was happening, it hadn't properly sunk in.

Staring at my empty bedroom, knowing it was the last time I'd see it, and realizing that London was no longer going to be the place I called home, I felt an overwhelming sadness.

I knew I had made the right decision in the long term, but the finality of it all came crashing over me like a tidal wave. I was no longer going to be regularly meeting up with Lucy and my whole life was about to change.

Living in London was an experience like no other. I know it sounds cheesy, but it really is where I learned so much about myself and what I could manage on my own.

And, if anyone had ever told me before that I'd end up working for a luxury fashion brand in their head offices, located in the heart of Soho, I would have laughed my head off and probably spat out my tea. Not me? But yet there I was, mingling with fashionistas and pretending I knew the difference between fuchsia and magenta. I might have only been there for three years, but in that time, I managed to achieve a lot for that company and, perhaps despite all the mishaps I kept myself alive.

I enjoyed the anonymity London had to offer, the fact that I could jump on a tube and go exploring, there was always somewhere new to discover, and I did that often.

I loved the diversity on my doorstep, from spending time mooching around the markets in East London or Camden, to strolling through one of the many parks scattered across the city.

I loved it all.

But it was time to move back to my parents. I was done with fucking about, drinking too much, partying too much and I craved being in the quieter town of Market Deeping and eventually moving to the city of Preston to be with my new love interest.

My best experiences of course, were undoubtedly, shared with my old mucka Lucy. The disastrous dating, the disgusting diets, the crazy nights out, or crazy nights in and the fact that we would find hilarity in any situation, good or bad. We created so many memories and I realised it was Lucy that was my biggest London experience.

I was sad to leave her behind, and there was no way I was going to lose touch with her. She knew far too fucking much.

And with that, I gathered my belongings into suitcases filled with memories of my London life. With each item carefully packed away, I embarked on the journey back to my teenage bedroom at my parents once again and leaving behind the bustling streets of London for a quieter new chapter for my life.

Chapter Twenty-Five

Studio Life

LUCY

As mentioned before, everything on Marie's vision board came true for her—she met a tall, dark-haired electrician and quickly fell in love. Her new relationship meant her boyfriend spent a lot of time at her house, which added urgency to my own goal of finding a job up North and moving to Manchester.

I tried to stay out of the house most evenings to give them space and would often leave London and visit friends or my parents on weekends. London had become solely a place of work for me, and I couldn't wait to leave.

In the week I would go to the pub within walking distance from Marie's house so they would have time alone together and not wanting to be a third wheel.

Whilst sitting alone one evening in the beer garden of the local pub, the sweetest little girl came over to me and started talking. 'Hello, my name is Phoebe, what's your name?'

She looked about eight years old and took a seat next to me.

Whilst talking to me she spilt my wine and with a panic on her face she said, 'I'm so sorry.' And ran off.

A few minutes later a tall, broad guy with an African accent came along with Phoebe and a younger boy and said, 'my daughter told me she has spilt your drink, please can I buy you a new one?'

I said 'Oh no don't worry, it's ok. I can go and get another one.' He insisted and bought me a new drink.

His name was Jack, and him and his children spent the next hour chatting away to me. We ended up swapping numbers and arranged to meet up the following evening.

Jack was about 40-something and was a single parent, who he had shared-custody of. He ran his own business and was smashing life as a single parent, his children adored him, and he was a fantastic father. He was also the sweetest, kindest man and I was excited about our new friendship.

Jack would cook dinner for me sometimes and I really enjoyed spending time with Jack and his children.

Jack was a lot older than me, but it did cross my mind at times that maybe this was fate, and this was perhaps who I should be with, but I was moving to Manchester, and I couldn't allow myself to meet anyone and fall for them.

His life was very 'sorted' and settled and mine was anything but that. But I proceeded to spend the weekdays mostly with Jack and his children.

When Marie's boyfriend was set to move in, I realized it was taking longer than expected to find a job in Manchester. Eventually, I found a studio flat in Enfield for £650 a month and moved in on a 6-month rental contract until I secured a job up North.

Living in the modern but very small flat turned out to be a challenge right from the start. The landlord's strict rule against wearing high heels on the flooring was particularly baffling to me—I lived in heels and couldn't imagine having to take them off before even entering the front door every day. It set an uncomfortable tone from the beginning.

As the months passed, the challenges only grew. I had zero heating in my studio flat, and at times, I could see my own breath in the cold air inside. Despite my repeated calls and emails to the letting agents, promises to fix these issues went unanswered. This left me feeling miserable, cold, and isolated in what was supposed to be my temporary sanctuary.

I'd also got this new neighbour who loved to chat every time we crossed paths on our floor.

So, one day in the flat carpark after coming home from work and I bumped into him. I casually dropped the bomb that it was my 27th birthday tomorrow. Instantly, he jumped into action and excitedly announced he had a present for me. Now, mind you, he had no clue it was my birthday just moments ago, but in a flash, he disappeared fast into his flat.

Moments after I stepped into my flat, there was a knock on my door, and like magic, there he stands with a box of chocolates in hand. I graciously thanked him and closed the door.

As I inspected the box, I noticed that there was no cellophane wrapping, and the box itself looked distressed. Curious, I lifted off the cardboard lid, only to find a half-eaten box of chocolates inside.

The following night, Kerrie came over to spend the evening with me. She knew I was feeling down and didn't want me to be alone on my birthday.

As Kerrie and I caught up, my chocolate-scoffing neighbour knocked on the door again, holding a bottle of wine and two glasses. Apparently, he was unaware that Kerrie was there, he must have assumed I was spending my birthday alone. Which would have been the case if not for Kerrie.

Despite the surprise and the misunderstanding, I didn't want to be impolite, so I welcomed him in. In my mind, I saw it as an opportunity to enjoy some free wine before we opened the bottles of wine that Kerrie and I had planned for the evening.

My new neighbour had a dramatic way of speaking, and Kerrie and I found the awkwardness of him sitting in on our evening quite amusing since we barely knew him.

To add to the surrealness of the situation, he suddenly decided to take his shirt off and casually sat on the sofa bare-chested.

I exchanged a bewildered glance with Kerrie, who appeared on the verge of bursting into uncontrollable laughter.

What the fuck does he want? A threesome? Is this his way of flirting? This couldn't get any weirder.

Despite the awkwardness, Kerrie and I struggled to contain our amusement, trying not to offend him whilst trying to contain our laughter.

He continued to sit there bare-chested, despite it being Autumn and not particularly warm, and considering I hadn't got any heating in my flat we were unsure why he did this. Kerrie and I tried to discreetly gulp down our wine, whilst he sipped his slowly, oblivious to overstaying his welcome.

Feeling increasingly uncomfortable, I realized that I needed to come-up with a plan to get him to leave.

I decided to tell him we had plans to go out and needed to get ready. However, he remained seated, prompting me to bluntly say, 'You need to go now so we can get ready, pleaseeeeeeee.'

I stood up, signalling that I was about to open the door for him to leave, but he still didn't budge.

Growing frustrated, I raised my voice a bit more firmly, 'You really need to go now.' Meanwhile, Kerrie pretended to be amused by a text message on her phone, although I knew she was actually trying not to burst out laughing at the weirdness of this situation.

Finally, he got the hint and reluctantly left. I slammed the door behind him, and we couldn't help but burst into giggles. I'm sure he heard us, but also very sure he probably didn't give a shit and was just trying his luck.

Back at work, Mr. Moon was my confidant and knew all about my plans to move to Manchester. He didn't want me to leave, and I didn't want to leave him either, but he understood my need to be near my parents again.

I worried about leaving Mr Moon. Mr. Moon's diet was notoriously bad; he often skipped meals throughout the day. I cared a lot about him, so I would bring him peanut butter on toast wrapped in tin foil for breakfast. Often, when I spent a weekend at my parents, my dad would prepare food for me to bring back for Mr. Moon, like a hearty chicken or beef stew filled with vegetables.

Mr. Moon loved it and was genuinely grateful. My Dad and I appreciated that he remained one of the sources of my happiness during my time in London and my dad knew how much I cared for Mr Moon and how I was concerned about his eating-habits.

Mr. Moon had a unique prediction about my love life—he was convinced that eventually, I would end up with a short, ginger-haired guy. He would often tell me, 'my friend Gina always dated tall, dark and handsome men and then ended up marrying a short, ginger guy. You will be exactly the same.' I wasn't so sure, but it made me think for a few seconds that I should expand beyond my usual type, looks-wise.

In the office, I got along really well with a guy named Doug. He was 6ft-something and had strawberry blonde hair, attractive, and even though he wasn't my usual type, I did have a soft spot for him. It was obvious to Mr Moon how well we got along.

So, whenever Mr. Moon spotted Doug and me talking, he would playfully hide behind a pillar so that I could see him, but Doug couldn't. He would put on a performance as if to suggest Doug and I should be kissing, his arms caressing the air as if orchestrating a dramatic and romantic kiss.

It always left me laughing on the inside, his immaturity for someone of manager status always had me in hysterics.

I knew that moving to Manchester meant giving up any hope of a future with Pump-it Pete and me, despite him lingering in the background for two years.

He had given me false hope at times, and I had been naive, hanging onto his every word. The final straw came when I told him about my plans to move, and all he said was, 'I will miss you, but I am happy for you.' Those words snapped me out of my two-year dee-loo-loo madness, and I knew I had to get over him.

There was once a time when I was 17 and really wanted a boyfriend. I wrote in my diary that weekend that I was going to go out, swap numbers with some guys, and give them a chance.

I exchanged numbers with three guys, and the one who I opted to go on a second date with wasn't chosen based on looks or status; it was simply because he was the only one who held the door of the pub open for me and acted like a gentleman the whole evening. We spent three years together.

This got me thinking back to my younger self—I had standards. I would never have put up with someone being half-arsed about me back then.

His lack of time and commitment should have given me the 'ick,' but nope, it ended up having quite the opposite effect.

I had never met anyone like him before, and I didn't want to lose him or the hope of a future eventually happening for us. I always believed he would eventually 'free-up' some time and again become the man I first met. I knew this wasn't normal. But at this point, I was ready—ready to give up this madness, even though it broke my heart to leave all hope behind.

I was very ready by now to move to Manchester. I just needed to snag a job, so I could pack my bags and get the hell outta London.

I loved my job in London, and I cherished my relationships with my colleagues, but without living with Layla, London didn't feel like home anymore.

Moving out from living with Layla was a decision I deeply regretted—it felt like my biggest mistake to date. They say the grass isn't always greener on the other side, but my new misery ultimately prompted me to make the decision to move closer to my parents.

In hindsight and with my new positive way of thinking, I realized that if I hadn't made the move to South London without Layla then Layla might not have met her boyfriend and moved back to her parents and later to Preston, Lancashire.

We would have more than likely remained content and happy living with one another in our cozy flat in Stoke Newington, neither of us would have likely considered leaving London behind.

It was a bittersweet realization—I missed our time together but understood the necessity of our separate journeys. It all happened for a reason.

Chapter Twenty-Six

KISS MY ARSE

April 2012

LUCY

After four months of living in Enfield in my little studio flat, I received an invitation for an interview at an advertising company near Trafford Park in Manchester, for a Business Development position. I couldn't believe it.

With my dad being given the all clear, he offered to drive me to my interview. I took the train from London to Derby, where my dad picked me up and drove me straight to Manchester.

At the interview, I met the owner of the business and one of the managers. The owner of the company was very humble, professional, and friendly with a good sense of humour—exactly my kind of boss.

I had to give a presentation on how I would develop their business, and I was extremely nervous. I had never worked in sales, but my parents convinced me that I was a people-person and could turn my hand to anything I wanted to.

The process took longer than anticipated, and at one point, the owner of the company invited my dad, who was waiting outside in the carpark, to come in and have a cup of tea while he waited.

It was a lovely gesture and warmed my heart, especially as they didn't know that he had been so poorly and the trauma he had gone through.

Also, being a people-person, my dad was delighted by their hospitality, and on the drive home after the interview, we both hoped I would get the job, not just for the role itself but also because the people seemed so lovely.

I returned to London ecstatic to have landed the job. Finally, I was set to leave London and move closer to my family, especially my parents.

Saying goodbye to Mr Moon was particularly tough; he was one of the funniest people I'd ever met and had become a dear friend. It was also bittersweet knowing I wouldn't see him every day anymore.

The first person I told after my parents was Layla. She shared that she had landed herself a clerical job, though not as glamorous as the fashion industry; she found herself working in the orthopaedics clinic at Royal Preston Hospital. She was incredibly happy with her boyfriend and settling into life in Preston.

I was so excited to soon be much closer to Layla – 45 minutes away as opposed to four hours. I could visit for the day, without the need to stay over.

My mum, dad and auntie kindly offered to help me hunt for a flat, knowing that I couldn't keep travelling back from London to search for a place to live. This was a huge relief.

With their assistance, I secured a two-bedroom flat in West Didsbury, Manchester, for a steal at £550 per month. It was a significant improvement from the tiny studio flat with no heating.

My Dad sent me photos and it looked very spacious compared to what I had in London. It had a bay window at the front and steps up to the flat, which made me feel like Carrie out of Sex and The City. I was very sure that this flat would inspire me to finally write a book.

I was on the ground floor. If this flat was located in London, then I would have been shitting myself, but as it was in West Didsbury, a nice area of Manchester, this didn't bother me.

I had a 4-week notice period for my current job and during this time I was giddy to be starting my new life near family and closer to my parents. My parents spent a lot of time in Manchester as it was due to my Mum's parents living there. So, I knew even when I wasn't visiting them in Belper, that I would see them so much more when they were visiting.

I told Jack and the girls, that I was moving, and we decided to have a farewell night down the pub one Friday evening. Jack being the gentleman that he was asked if I needed any help moving but I declined. My parents were coming down in a hire van and helping me to move.

The farewell Friday evening with Jack and his children, was incredibly emotional. Not for me, but for Jack. He was crying his eyes out, and I felt incredibly bad. I didn't realise I meant so much to him. I'm very sure Pump-it Pete hadn't shed a tear after I told him I was leaving and there Jack was crying that he would miss me so much.

The night continued with the music blaring in the pub. 'Champagne Supernova' by Oasis started playing, and Jack enthusiastically grabbed my hand, lifting it into the air as if we were at a concert. He sang at the top of his lungs, tears streaming down his face. Soon, all four of us joined hands, swaying and singing along, our arms swinging from left to right.

In that moment, a wave of sadness washed over me about leaving London. Up until then, I had been riding high on cloud nine, but in that moment I began to realize that the life I had built there after Layla left wasn't so bad after all. I started feeling immensely grateful for the opportunity to meet everyone along the way. It dawned on me—I was truly going to miss this life. It had changed me in ways I couldn't have imagined.

From meeting incredible people to learning about things like Orthodox Judaism, majesty's pleasure, to remember to always have air freshener and a plunger in your bathroom, from navigating sticky situations and emerging unscathed, to the laughter shared with Layla and the lessons learned about love—especially about never settling for someone who couldn't offer me what I deserved—it all flooded my mind.

Leaving London was bittersweet, but as I reflected on the journey and the people who had become a part of my life, I knew I was carrying with me memories and lessons that would shape my future wherever I went.

Moving day had finally arrived, and my parents had left ahead with all my belongings in the van bound for Manchester. I stayed behind to finish cleaning and drop off the flat keys at the letting agency.

As I left Enfield in my car, a wave of sadness and nervousness washed over me. Was this the right decision? But, it was too late to question it.

Driving onto the motorway, I popped in my Adele CD and played her song '*Someone Like You*' on repeat. Singing along to the lyrics, tears streamed down my face. '*I heard that you're settled down. That you found a girl and you're married now. I heard that your dreams came true. Guess she gave you things, I didn't give to you.'*

The emotions overwhelmed me as I pictured returning to London years later, perhaps visiting Pump-it Pete at his gym as a surprise and then finding out that he was happily married. But then it hit me—I needed to let go, to release him from my thoughts. Sobbing even harder, I sang at the top of my lungs, *'Never mind, I will find someone like you. I wish nothing but the best for you, too. Don't forget me, I beg.'*

With each verse, I was trying to release him from my system, singing harder and harder. It was time to move forward, leaving behind what could have been and embracing what lay ahead in Manchester. And so, I kept singing louder and louder in the hope this was some type of car karaoke exorcism to get him out of my head.

Tears streamed down my face, and I glanced at the car mirror. My reflection showed a blotchy mess, snorting and sobbing uncontrollably.

Up until that moment, I had been angry with him—for his apparent lack of emotion, for not seeming to care that I was leaving. It felt like he either didn't give a shit or hadn't even registered that I was leaving.

Why had I fallen so hard for someone who couldn't reciprocate the same level of commitment? These thoughts swirled in my mind as Adele's song echoed through the car, and whilst I was trying to get rid of the ache in my heart.

As I neared Manchester, I managed to calm down. Kerrie was on her way from Market Deeping to lend a hand with settling into my new flat. My auntie who lived close by was also going to meet my parents and I there to help with unpacking. I desperately didn't want anyone to see me in that emotional state—I wanted this move to be a fresh and exciting start in my life.

I wiped away my tears, took deep breaths, and tried to compose myself before they arrived. This was supposed to be a day of new beginnings, not one where I had been performing my own exorcism to release emotions from the past.

I pulled over in a street around the corner from my new flat and reapplied my make-up, my eyes were puffy, but I thought that I could potentially get away with it. I continued driving and was ready to commence my new life.

As I pulled up to my new flat, everyone who was helping me move was already there.

But when moving my items into the flat we ran into a snag when we discovered that my sofa wouldn't fit through the lounge's heavy wooden fire doors. Without hesitation, Kerrie reassured us, saying, 'Don't panic, I'll get my toolbox from the car.' I was so grateful she was there.

She marched off confidently, returning with her toolbox as if she were Bob the Builder herself. Climbing onto my computer chair that had been brought in from the van, she expertly started unscrewing the bolts from the fire doors.

My auntie found this all quite amusing; she had never seen a woman so confident with a toolkit. Being raised by her dad, Kerrie had always been one of the handiest friends I had. Nothing DIY ever fazed her.

I fell in love with my flat on Clyde Road as soon as I saw it in person. I knew I was going to feel settled there. It had a good vibe and was conveniently located around the corner from plenty of bars, pubs and restaurants.

It was a bit dangerous being so close to so many bars and pubs, but hey, Layla wasn't there, so I knew that I wouldn't fall trap back into the party lifestyle and get as smashed as we used to together. This was a classy place to live, and I intended to act accordingly. They say you're a product of your environment, right?

I wasted no time getting to know the local pubs. The following day, I had some afternoon drinks with a DJ that I had met years ago, he lived in Manchester, and we had kept in touch over the years.

After the drinks I stumbled back tipsy to my flat, I knew I had a bottle of red wine waiting for me to enjoy in front of the TV that evening, which topped off a great afternoon.

Whilst watching TV, my phone pings. It was Pump-it Pete.

Hey babe, are you in Manchester now? I miss you so badly. I don't want to do life without you. It will be different this time. I can't lose you. Can we get back together? We can make it work. xxxxxx

Whilst in London those were the words that I had desperately yearned to hear.

But when they finally came, instead of joy, I was seething with anger and spat out words under my breath that my mum would not be proud of.

'This new classy me can stay on ice right now,' I thought. With wine flowing through my blood, I frantically found a picture on Google of an old man's hairy arse crack, I sent the picture accompanied by a text as my frustration was boiling over.

Kiss my arse! You had your chance, and now that I'm four hours away, you suddenly want to commit to me again? Not happening. I don't believe you and I never will. Leave me alone.

'That will show him,' I thought.

I finally figured it out, I was his placeholder for two years until he figured out what he wanted, but no more. It was also my fault. I showed him how he could treat me, and I allowed him to treat me that way.

Manchester was my fresh-start, and I didn't want to waste any more of my time on him. They say getting back with an ex is like re-reading the same story and knowing the ending, and I certainly wasn't going to put myself through that all over again.

It felt good to finally have my blinkers off. I knew from that moment forward that it was much much better to be alone, than to settle for someone who had made me feel alone.

I might have been 27-years old, but I was proud of the hairy arse crack picture and thought I was being rather unique. I was very adamant that the picture made it abundantly clear that I was not happy, and I was not going to let him mess me around ever again.

In a fit of defiance, I scribbled his number on a piece of paper and stashed it away in my underwear drawer—just in case I had a weak moment to change my mind and message him.

Then, I deleted his number from my phone, determined never to be tempted to reach out to him. It was a declaration of independence, a closure I needed to move on.

The car exorcism worked. It was a bloody miracle. I sank the rest of my wine and fell asleep content with knowing I did the right thing in cutting it completely dead in its tracks before I wasted another two years on that man.

The following day I cruised down West Didsbury high street to get familiar with the area, I did a courteous thing and flashed my lights to let a bus pull out.

The driver lifted his hand and gave me a grateful wave. Bloody Nora, this was unfamiliar territory for me.

Still buzzing with surprise, I immediately called Kerrie, exclaiming, 'A bus driver just thanked me!'

Living in London had made me accustomed to people going about their daily lives, with no fucks given to raise a hand to suggest a thank you, well not in my experience anyway - this small act of appreciation and friendliness felt like a revelation, and I knew my personality would be more suited to the friendliness and slower pace of life that Manchester had to offer.

The first week at my new job was going really well. I had my own chuffing office! I had never had my own office before; gosh, I felt important.

I got along well with two girls in particular, who were just my sort of vibe. They were fun and ambitious, and I just knew I was going to be happy there.

The owner of the company was still just as lovely as when I first met him. He was chilled and got along with all his staff. People seemed really happy, and the good vibes rubbed off.

I text Layla that day to let her know that the move to Manchester went well, that I was enjoying my job and I suggested that we meet up as soon as I was settled.

I'm so excited for you chick! I cannot wait to see you and so happy everything is going well. Long story, but I am single again. I've got to move out in one week. When can we catch up? xxx

Without a second thought, I called Layla and invited her to live with me in Manchester.

Just like old times, we would be flatmates again, ready to tackle life's twists and turns together. Back to dating and navigating our way through new adventures—but this time, up North.

Printed in Great Britain
by Amazon